Going

Deeper

McDougal & Associates
Servants of Christ and Stewards of the
Mysteries of God

Going Deeper

A 90-Day Devotional

by

Crystal Callais

Going Deeper
Copyright © 2020 — Crystal Callais
ALL RIGHTS RESERVED

Published by:

Mcdougal & Associates

18896 Greenwell Springs RD
Greenwell Springs, LA 70739
www.thepublishedword.com

McDougal & Associates is dedicated to spreading the Gospel
of the Lord Jesus Christ to as many people as possible
in the shortest time possible.

ISBN 978-1-950398-19-5

Printed in the U.S., the U.K. and Australia
For Worldwide Distribution

Dedication

This book is dedicated to you, the reader. My heart for you is that, as you read the following pages, God will speak directly to your heart, bringing you on your journey with Him. I pray that the Father sparks something inside of you to make you want to go deeper, deeper in your relationship with Him, deeper in your relationship with others, deeper in your understanding of the Word of God, deeper in heart revelation and obedience to Him.

Acknowledgments

I would like to give thanks to God for the revelations I personally received in my quiet time with Him. I'm grateful for the opportunity and the ability to write what I received in my own life in a way that encourages others in their relationship with the Father. The journey God has taken me on in this process has forever changed my life!

I would also like to acknowledge those who helped with the encouragement, editing and forming of this book:

- Russell Callais, my husband and forever friend. Thank you for encouraging me to keep going and to share my heart with others. Thank you for the time you spent to help me gather my thoughts. Thank you for believing in me! I love you!
- Kurt and Lorraine Foret, my parents. Thank you for believing in me. You have instilled in me that with God all things are possible. You have helped me to dream and not limit myself. Thank you for encouraging me along the way!
- Kim and Vanessa Voisin, my pastors. Thank you for seeing what God was doing in our life and nurturing that within us. Thank you for being obedient

to the Father and helping us walk through the opportunities God has opened in our life. Over the last twenty years you both have spoken into our lives and the lives of our children and imparted many things to us. We are forever grateful for having such amazing shepherds.

- My siblings and my children: Thank for believing in me and helping me dream. Thank you for encouraging me to keep going!
- The countless friends and mentors who speak into my life: Thank you for encouraging me to be real when I'm talking and writing. I'm grateful for your friendship and belief in me to keep reaching and to allow God to work and shine in my life.

> *And the* LORD *answered me, and said,*
> *Write the vision, and make it plain upon*
> *tables, that he may run that readeth it.*
>
> Habakkuk 2:2

My heartcry is that the words in this book, derived from my revelations and visions, are written plain enough that they inspire others to read and then run with their own revelations of God's Word.

Contents

Foreword by
Rev. Kim Voisin, Ph.D.

Crystal Callais invites her readers to go deeper, while shedding light on many Bible passages that create discovery. She challenges you to break through old paradigms that have been created from past experiences and may not even line up with biblical teaching. This journal will draw out the best in a person's character of honesty, kinship, purity, grace, holiness and beliefs. You will be challenged on how you relate to God and one another, and in all your relationships. I highly recommend it, having seen the fruits of it in our congregation.

Rev. Kim F. Voisin
Vision Christian Center
Bourg, Louisiana

Foreword by Pastor J.D. Smith

Going Deeper: Swimming in the shallows allows most people to skim along, barely seeing or experiencing a portion of all there is, while those diving deeper get extraordinary views. *Going Deeper* is harder, yet it offers greater rewards!

Amazing rewards are available in this new release by Crystal Callais. As she dives deeper with you, strategically guiding the way in God's Holy Word, you will see so much more of the greatness of God and your unlocked potential to live fully free.

Get copies for yourself, your family, your friends and even your enemies, and then take a dive, *Going Deeper*, only to rise again and soar!

JD Smith
Pastor/Founder CitiIMPACT Ministries
Founder, JDSmithOnline.com

Introduction

This devotional was inspired to help strengthen your walk with God. It is meant to be read alongside of your Bible. Daily devotional time in God's Word will change your heart and your reality.

Joshua 1:8

> *This book of the law shall not depart out of thy mouth; but thou shalt meditate therein day and night, that thou mayest observe to do according to all that is written therein: for then thou shalt make thy way prosperous, and then thou shalt have good success.*

This devotional is designed to help guide you into a deeper walk with God. Here's what to look for:

1. Each devotion is titled with a quick summary of the topic you will read about that day.

2. On each beginning page, you will see a place for you to write in what you are thankful for. Psalm 100:4 declares: *"Enter into his gates with thanksgiving, and into his courts with praise:*

be thankful unto him, and bless his name." Make it a habit to start your day being thankful to God. This will set your atmosphere to hear from God and to see into His Word.

3. You will find one or more scriptures references to read. I have used several popular versions for these readings (the King James Version, the Amplified Bible, The Message and the Passion Translation). It is a good idea to study from several different translations. This helps you to have a better understanding of what the Scriptures are saying.

4. The Scriptures are broken down and, in some instances, examples are given to help you relate the Word of God to your own everyday life.

5. To end your daily devotional time, you will see some questions under the title **"Ask Yourself."** This will help you make the Word applicable to your personal life, so that you can have the deeper relationship with Christ that you desire.

6. Finally, you will find, at the end of each devotional, a challenge for prayer, something from the day's teaching to take to God and then to listen for His answer.

As you read these daily devotions, you are encouraged to:

1. Get a notebook and write out your answers to the questions put forth.

2. Open your heart and your spiritual ears and write down anything else the Lord reveals to you during this time in His presence.

3. Finally, write a prayer to God. This will help you apply what you have read to your own situation. The more you apply the Word to your heart personally the more you will see yourself growing, *GOING DEEPER.*

My desire for you is that you go deeper! The more time you spend in God's Word, the thirstier for the Word you will become. Every time you open His Word and apply it to your life, you will grow. God will stir a thirst in you to become all that He has ordained for your life. He said:

Jeremiah 1:5
Before I formed thee in the belly I knew thee; and before thou camest forth out of the womb I sanctified thee, and I ordained thee a prophet unto the nations.

℘ DAY 1 ℘

What Report Do I Believe?

Today, I am thankful for: _____

_____

_____

Today's Scripture Reading Is Numbers 13:1-33 and 14:6-10

Moses chose twelve men to send to spy out the land of Canaan, one from each of the twelve tribes of Israel. These twelve men went and spied out the land for forty days, and, at the end of those forty days, returned to Moses with their reports. From the majority of the spies, the report was not good. Ten of the men reported, "The land was indeed full of milk, honey and fruit, but the people are strong, and the cities are walled."

As they were giving out this negative report, Caleb quieted them down and said, "Let's go conquer the land. We are more than able to do it."

The other men countered Caleb with more negative reporting. They talked of how big and strong the other people were and how small they saw themselves. In verse 33 of the King James Version, they said, *"We were IN OUR*

OWN SIGHT *as grasshoppers, and SO WE WERE IN THEIR SIGHT."* (Emphasis Mine)

What the Israelites believed about themselves dictated their reality. How they saw themselves in their own sight was what they became in the Amalekites' sight. What they believed about themselves dictated their future! And what you believe about yourself will dictate your future as well.

The only spies who believed differently were Caleb, from Judah's lineage, and Joshua. What do you tend to believe and run with? A negative report? Or a positive report?

Ask Yourself

- When I am asked about a situation I'm facing, do I see it in a negative light or a positive one?
- Do I see how big the giants are or how big my God is?
- God has the Promised Land for every one of us. Am I willing to fight the enemy to get in? Or do I bow in fear, because of what I "THINK" he has against me?
- If what I believe about myself dictates my reality, what *do* I believe?

_____

_____

_____

_____

Pray and ask God to help you see the positive report in your situation. Ask Him to help you see yourself like Caleb, able to conquer the enemy and not as a grasshopper.

✒ DAY 2 ✒

Do I Keep My Word?

Today, I am thankful for: _____

_____

_____

Today's Scripture Reading Is
Deuteronomy 23:21-23

When thou shalt vow a vow unto the LORD thy God, thou shalt not slack to pay it: for the LORD thy God will surely require it of thee; and it would be sin in thee. But if thou shalt forbear to vow, it shall be no sin in thee. That which is gone out of thy lips thou shall keep and perform; even a freewill offering, according as thou hast vowed unto the LORD thy God, which thou has promised with thy mouth.

God was saying that if you make a vow and don't keep your word, you have sinned. Whatever goes out of your lips, you are required to do, *"even a freewill offering."* Your free will is found in your soul and is part of your emotional being. You can choose to do or not to do. It is a voluntary act of your words and deeds. Even if you speak a vow or promise out of emotion, you are required to walk out what you have said.

How many times do we break our word because we make idle conversation? How often do we not mean what we say? We tend to talk so lightly that we don't even remember what we have committed ourselves to? But God holds us to our words. How many times do we break our word, even to God? We promise to do certain things, if God opens the door. Then the door opens, and we don't do what we have promised. God considers this to be sin.

Ask Yourself:

- Do I do what I say I will do?
- Am I dependable to people and/or to God for keeping my word?
- Do I make promises or commitments (even out of emotion) and then don't keep them?
- What thing (vow) have I spoken and not followed through with that God is now convicting me of?

_____

_____

_____

_____

_____

Pray and allow God to bring back to your remembrance things you may have promised or committed to and have not completed. Ask for forgiveness and start making efforts to keep your word. Ask God to remind you of your most recent commitment and then keep it!

✥ **DAY 3** ☜

Do I Pay My Vows?

Today, I am thankful for: _____

_____

_____

Today's Scripture Reading Is
Psalm 66:13-20

In my Bible, these scriptures are under a heading called "Worship the Lord." The writer expresses:

I will go into thy house with burnt offerings: I will pay thee my vows, which my lips have uttered, and my mouth hath spoken, when I was in trouble.   Verses 13-14

The worshipper then offers his sacrifices with incense. He was referring to making a promise to God. The Scriptures teach us that when we bring our gift to the altar and we remember our *"ought,"* we should go and make it right. In Psalms, the *"ought"* is referring to vows or promises we make in the heat of trouble. What if the "ought" you have is with God?

Maybe you have said things like:

If You heal me, I will ... .
If this was paid off, I would ... .
If I had more time, I would ... .
If You would change this person, then ... .
If You would give me a better job, then ... .

Ask Yourself

- What vows have I made to God that I broke?
- Do I keep my end of the words or bargains I've made?
- What impulsive things do I say when I am in trouble or in a stressful situation?

_____

_____

_____

_____

_____

_____

_____

_____

Spend some time allowing God to bring back to your remembrance things you have said that you did not then carry though with. Maybe it's time to do them and make it right.

✗ DAY 4 ✗

What Are My Actions When Faced with Temptation?

Today, I am thankful for: _____

_____

_____

Today's Scripture Reading Is
Psalm 141:1-10

This is a psalm of David, a prayer he prayed when he was facing temptation. There are a few key points that I want to make:

- In verse 3, David asked God to guard his lips, not to let him speak impulsively.
- In verse 4, he asked God not to let his heart incline to any evil thing.
- In verse 9, he asked God to keep him from the snares that men had set before him, the bait of iniquity. He was praying against the temptation before him because he knew it had a root in his heart.

When Jesus faced His accusers, He held His peace (see Matthew 26:57-68). When I am faced with false accusations against me, am I tempted to defend myself rather than let God defend me? Do I pray for God to help guard my lips?

David didn't pray for God to make him stronger. He didn't pray that God would change his circumstances. He didn't pray that God would even remove the temptation from him. The sum of his prayer was for God to teach him and help him with self-control.

According to Galatians 5:23, *temperance*, which is self-control, is one of the fruits of the Spirit. This means we all have a form of self-control as a seed within. David was faced with something, and he was choosing in that moment to look inside of himself. Do you look within?

Ask Yourself

- What are my temptations?
- When faced with a temptation, do I automatically pray for it to leave?
- Do I ask myself why this thing even tempts me?
- Do I knowingly put myself in front of the temptation?
- What do I believe I will receive from the temptation if I give in to it?

_____

_____

_____

_____

Pray that God will show you why certain things are a temptation to you. Pray that He shows you the root and the stronghold it has on you, so that you can be free from it.

✄ DAY 5 ☞

Do I Feel Alone?

Today, I am thankful for: _____

_____

_____

Today's Scripture Reading Is
Psalm 142:1-7, 1ˢᵗ Samuel 22:1-23 and 24:1-22

David was hiding from Saul in a cave. Saul went into the cave to rest, and suddenly David had the opportunity to kill his tormentor. Instead, David just cut off the corner of Saul's robe. David was not alone in that cave. He had six hundred men who followed him. Why, then, in Psalm 142, did he say, *"there was no man that would know me"* and *"no man cared for my soul"* (verse 4).

In that cave, the men with David were telling him that this was his chance to kill Saul, but David refused to kill God's anointed. He didn't feel like his men were even on his side in that moment although in his heart he knew that was wrong. They were right in that he did have the opportunity to kill Saul and could have called it self-defense.

Let's apply this storyline to our lives today: When you are being chased down by false accusations, and someone is trying to kill your reputation, how do you respond? Do you react, jump in and kill their reputation when you get the chance? Or do you leave it in God's hands? In the physical, David was being set up by the enemy to kill Saul, but he refused to fall into that trap. God knows where we are and that there are snares set before us. The enemy of our soul knows it too.

David looked to his right, and his men were not protecting him from the snare of the enemy. He then told God: *"Thou art my refuge and my portion in the land of the living"* (verse 5).

Ask Yourself

- When I feel cornered and pursued by the enemy, do I look to people as a refuge or to God?
- Even though I may be surrounded by people, do I feel alone?
- Do I feel that no one will understand?
- Do I feel that no one really knows my struggle?
- Do I feel judged?
- Do I believe more in reality, man, or God as my refuge? And why?

_____

_____

_____

_____

Pray and ask God to show you the truth that lies within your heart. He is standing with you in the cave. If you feel alone, ask Him to reveal the reason for it.

❧ DAY 6 ❧

Have I Prepared for Tomorrow?

Today, I am thankful for: _____

_____

_____

Today's Scripture Reading Is
Joshua 3:5

And Joshua said unto the people, Sanctify yourselves: for tomorrow the LORD will do wonders among you.

Joshua told the Israelites to sanctify themselves that day so that God could move among them the next. In the same way that God had parted the Red Sea for Moses to cross, He was about to part the Jordan River for them to cross (see chapters 3 and 4). But notice that they had to prepare "today" so God could do His miracle "*tomorrow.*"

We all pray for miracles to happen in our lives. Whether it is a financial breakthrough, someone getting saved or even a healing to take place, we seem to have this scripture backwards. We wonder why God has not answered our prayers and come through for us, but have we prepared ourselves for His miracle?

We pray for the miracle first; then we'll get our life right. We pray for God to give us a financial breakthrough first; then we'll tithe. We pray for God to give us a healing; then we'll eat right or take better care of ourselves. We pray for God to miraculously do something with our kids or our spouse; then we will do what is required of us.

As an example of how we could be applying this scripture backwards, let's say that you are praying that your spouse will get saved. But, then, when someone asks about your spouse, you speak negatively of them. "He'll never change" or "that's just the way he is." We are waiting for God to move today so that we can clean up our speech tomorrow. But, no, we must sanctify ourselves today. We must allow God to clean up our heart and separate us unto Him TODAY. This gives Him something to work with in our life for tomorrow's breakthrough.

Ask Yourself

- Do I wait for God to move before I clean up my words or actions?
- What needs to be sanctified in me today, so that God can move tomorrow?

_____

_____

_____

_____

_____

Ask God to show you where you need to be set apart and cleaned up. Ask Him to show you how to start applying this scripture the correct way, instead of backwards, in your daily life.

⌀ **DAY 7** ⌀

What's In My Heart?

Today, I am thankful for: _____

_____

_____

Today's Scripture Reading Is
Proverbs 4:20-23

We often hear quoted, *"Keep [guard] thy heart with all diligence; for out of it are the issues of life"* (verse 23). This being true, if we don't like our reality, we must look at our heart with open eyes. Proverbs presents us a process for changing our heart:

"Attend to my words; incline thine ear unto my sayings" (Verse 20). In other words, heed God's warnings by turning your ear to hear Him. And you can only heed and hear God's Word if you know God's Word.

"Let them not depart from thine eyes; keep them in the midst of thine heart" (Verse 21). In other words, don't let the words just come into your mind; guard them in your heart and do what you read. Your mind (what you believe and think) must line up and become one with your heart.

"For they are life unto those that find them, and health to their flesh" (Verse 22). This "they" refers to the Words of God. They are life and health to those who find them, but they are only life and health if they make it into your heart.

"Keep thy heart with all diligence; for out of it are the issues of life" (Verse 23). In other words, your heart holds the issues that manifest in your reality!

Look at the steps this scripture shows for you to take so that life and healing can manifest in your reality:

1. Heed and submit to God's Word.
2. Apply and do the Word, not just hear it.
3. If you submit and apply the Word, it then becomes life and healing to you.
4. It brings life and healing BECAUSE it's now a part of your heart. You speak from the abundance of your heart, and you eat the fruit of your lips.

Ask Yourself

- What is the condition of my heart?
- I speak life and death. So, if I HONESTLY listen to my speech, is my heart healthy or sick?

_____

_____

_____

Pray that God would show you how to change the condition of your heart. This will cause life and healing to manifest in your reality!

⚡ **DAY 8** ⚡

Do I Gossip?

Today, I am thankful for: _____

_____

_____

Today's Scripture Reading Is Proverbs 18:8

The words of a talebearer are AS WOUNDS, and they go down into the innermost parts of the belly.

The words of gossip merely REVEAL THE WOUNDS OF HIS OWN SOUL and his slander penetrates into the innermost being. (TPT)

According to Proverbs, we gossip because of the hurts we hold on to in life. Gossip shows me and others my internal wounds. It can also show me the wounds of others, if I am looking and not judging them for their gossip.

Gossip is our way of crying out for help. We are telling others where we are hurting, and we don't even realize it. As Christians, we tend to judge and avoid those in and out of church who gossip. We stay away from them by classifying them. In reality, they are the ones who are spiritually sick and crying out. It's time that we stop avoiding these people. We need to stop listening to their talebearing and start praying for them. It's easy to judge others for gossip, but turn the mirror on yourself for a minute.

Ask Yourself

- What do I spend my time talking about?
- What is the one thing I struggle with that causes me to run off at the mouth?
- Is there a wound I haven't let go of that is in the process of forming in my spirit man?

_____

_____

_____

_____

_____

_____

_____

_____

Ask God to heal your wounds. When you hear gossip, start praying for the person who is spreading it and ask God to heal them.

⚡ **DAY 9** ⚡

Who Does My Disobedience Affect?

Today, I am thankful for: _____

_____

_____

Today's Scripture Reading Is
Jonah 1:1-7

God called Jonah to go to Nineveh, and Jonah made a conscious decision to disobey. Verse 3 says, *"Jonah rose up to flee unto Tarshish FROM THE PRESENCE OF THE LORD."* His disobedience to God's direction put distance between him and God. God never left Jonah; Jonah left God's presence.

The result was that the Lord sent a great storm after Jonah. All the men traveling on the ship with him were afraid and began reaching out to their gods, but even during such a tumultuous storm, Jonah was asleep at the bottom of the ship. The others woke him up and told him to reach out to his God for help. The Scriptures say that they then decided to cast lots (something they believed in), and God used that method to call Jonah out.

Jonah's disobedience had caused the storm, and yet the storm didn't affect only him; It also affected others around him.

The fact that Jonah was sleeping through the storm may indicate that his conscience didn't bother him. But God's love pursues us even in our disobedience. He sent the storm because of Jonah's actions, and it was Jonah's fault that the ship was being tossed about. There are times in our life when we go through storms, and some of those storms come because of our disobedience. How many times do we blame God or others when it has actually been our own fault? Jonah's actions put other people's lives in danger.

How was it possible for Jonah to be numb to conviction? We can become numb to conviction out of anger, unforgiveness or our own walls of protection.

Ask Yourself

- What causes me to be disobedient to God?
- When storms or pressure come, do I automatically blame God or others? Do I even consider looking at myself as the cause?
- What excuses do I use to justify my actions when I'm numb to conviction?
- Have others spoken to me about possible storms because God is trying to get my attention?

_____

_____

Ask God to allow you to see the reason for your storm. Pray that your convictions would grow stronger and you would not become numb to the nudging of the Spirit.

✄ **DAY 10** ✄

Do I Have Heart Knowledge?

Today, I am thankful for: _____

_____

_____

Today's Scripture Reading Is Jonah 1:8-17

Jonah was asked by the shipmaster to identify himself and his occupation, and his response was: *"I am an Hebrew and I fear the LORD the God of heaven"* (verse 9). The men who heard this were afraid and asked him why he had fled from the presence of the Lord. Why did that catch the sailors' attention?

Jonah said he feared God (those were his words), but he had fled from God because he didn't want to do what was being asked of him (those were his actions). Clearly his words and his actions didn't line up. The sailors caught that and because they believed the storm was his fault, they didn't know what to do with him.

Jonah said he feared God, but his actions proved that to be false. If he feared God, he wouldn't have been disobedient. He may have had head knowledge of fearing God, but in his heart, he did not fear God. If he had, his actions would have been different. God had to do something to bring Jonah from head knowledge to heart knowledge.

The sailors tried everything in their power to get their ship to land but couldn't. They ended up throwing Jonah in the water, and then the storm stopped. I love verse 16: *"Then the men feared the* LORD *exceedingly, and offered a sacrifice unto the* LORD, *and made vows."* God used Jonah's disobedience to turn others to Himself. All of God's judgements are redemptive in nature, that is they are meant to reconcile us back to Him. The judgment that came for Jonah's disobedience wasn't just to reconcile *him* back to God, but also to redeem those sailors as well.

When Jonah hit the water, he didn't die. God still wanted to use him to reach Nineveh. Our actions don't change God's mind about us. He had arranged for a great fish to swallow Jonah and still he didn't die. God was giving Jonah an open door out of the judgment, giving him time to repent and return to Him.

Ask Yourself

- What judgements or storms am I facing?
- What head knowledge of God do I have that the storm I'm facing needs to change to heart knowledge?
- Since God never gives us more than we can handle, and He gave Jonah an open door to make things right, where is my open door?

_____

_____

Thank God for the heart knowledge you have received and are about to receive.

⚡ DAY 11 ⚡

Am I Honest with Myself and God?

Today, I am thankful for: _____

_____

_____

Today's Scripture Reading Is
Jonah 2:1-10

Jonah prayed from the belly of the great fish. *"I cried by reason of mine affliction unto the Lord, and he heard me"* (Verse 2). Jonah had to admit that the storm that put everyone's life in danger was his fault. Then he proceeded to tell God everything that he had been through in the next few verses. Notice that this did not move God. Then there was a shift, and a very significant change took place in Jonah.

"When my soul fainted within me, I remembered the LORD" (Verse 7). *"I will sacrifice unto thee with the voice of thanksgiving; I will pay that that I vowed"* (Verse 9). It was not until Jonah's emotions and impulse had faded that he was able to realize what needed to be done. As soon as he realized it, the very next verse says that God spoke to the fish to spit Jonah out on dry land.

My outward works that seem holy are not the things that move God. Jonah knew in his heart what he needed to do to get in right standing with His Creator. He had to sacrifice himself joyfully and then do what he said he would do. He had to obey and go to Nineveh.

How many times do we pray, "God use me to change the community, workplace, school, city or country? God, use me, I'm a willing vessel." But when God begins to speak to us, it's not what we have pictured. Jonah didn't understand why God would show mercy to the people of Nineveh, for Nineveh had a bad reputation, and Jonah didn't think the inhabitants deserved God's mercy.

Ask Yourself

- Am I a willing vessel to be used by God, only if and when I like the way He plans to use me?
- Do I emotionally pray, "Use me anywhere You want," and then change my mind, ending up with broken vows like Jonah?
- Is my prayer to God emotional or intentional?
- Am I honest with God (or even with myself) about why I feel the way I do?

_____

_____

_____

_____

Ask God to give you the strength to endure what you are going through and the strength to do what you have said you will do. Learn to pray intentionally and honestly.

❦ DAY 12 ❧

Do I Have Works with My Faith?

Today, I am thankful for: _____

_____

_____

Today's Scripture Reading Is Jonah 3:1-10 and James 2:14-26

The word of the Lord came to Jonah a second time saying, *"Go unto Nineveh"* (verse 2). This time Jonah made his way to Nineveh to warn the people of destruction that God said was coming in forty days. But, when the people of Nineveh heard Jonah's warning, they believed. The king sent out a decree telling all the people to fast, put on sackcloth (which signified repentance), cry out to God and turn from their evil ways. God saw their works, that they had turned from their evil ways. **I want you to examine this breakdown:**

- The king calling for a fast showed spiritual action. His telling the people to put on sackcloth showed a physical action.

- The king telling them to turn from their evil ways showed a spiritual action. Telling them to stop the violence of their hands showed a physical action.
- God saw their works (their physical action) and that they had turned from their evil (their spiritual action).

These people applied what Jonah was saying to their hearts and allowed God to do heart surgery on them. Do we allow God's Word to come in and circumcise our hearts? James declared: *"Faith without works is dead"* (James 2:20). The king's work showed his faith. Jonah 3:9 says, *"Who can tell if God will turn and repent."* They didn't know for sure that if God would change His mind about the judgment, but they acted with faith anyway. Then, when God looked upon them, He saw their works and their faith behind the works. What does God see when He looks at you?

Ask Yourself

- Is there fruit behind my faith?
- Has a heart change taken place in me, or am I just going through the motions?
- What type of fruit do my actions show?

_____

_____

_____

_____

Pray that God will do heart surgery on you and show you where you have faith without works.

❦ DAY 13 ❧

What Is On My Heart?

Today, I am thankful for: _____

_____

_____

Today's Scripture Reading Is
Jonah 4:1-11

When Jonah got angry because people who didn't deserve God's mercy were reaping His mercy, God asked him, "Why are you angry?" Jonah proceeded to blame God: "I knew You would give mercy, but they don't deserve mercy, and that is why I fled." Then he went outside of the city and sat down, to watch and see if the city would be destroyed.

Notice that God gave Jonah shade to keep him out of the heat and deliver him from his grief. This made Jonah happy. Then God sent a worm to eat the plant that had shaded him, and that made Jonah angry again. Now there was an extreme heat, but God used this plant as a parable to show Jonah how much He cared for the people of Nineveh.

Put yourself in Jonah's place. How often do you find yourself sitting on the sidelines waiting to see someone reap judgment instead of mercy? Do you get angry when people don't get what you think they deserve? Do you receive from God what you deserve? None of us do and all because of everything Jesus did for us on Calvary.

Notice that in the entire story of Jonah Satan is not mentioned even one time. God sent the storm, the worm and the heat. How often do we say we are doing what God wants by being obedient and yet insist, "Satan is attacking me," the minute we encounter hard times? Satan never attacked Jonah. God was trying to get Jonah to have a heart for people, to reap mercy, and to be willing to be used by Him with the right motive.

Ask Yourself

- When things go wrong and I'm technically obeying God and doing what He asked, even if inside I don't want to, do I automatically rebuke Satan for attacking me?
- Do I stop to ask God if He is sending pressure my way to get my attention?
- When I repeatedly circle the mountain of my life, do I choose to learn what is causing it so that I can stop the cycle?
- Do I sit on the sidelines and wait for people to reap judgment or mercy?
- What if I perceive them as an enemy? Do I still want them to reap mercy?

_____

_____

Pray that God would show you where your heart truly lies. Pray that your eyes would be opened to clearly see the storm. Is God shaking you? Or is it really an attack from Satan?

✂ DAY 14 ✄

Am I God-Centered or People-Centered?

Today, I am thankful for: _____

_____

_____

Today's Scripture Reading Is Galatians 1:10

For do I now persuade men, or God? or do I seek to please men? for if I yet pleased men, I should not be the servant of Christ.

This verse is presented in the context of preaching the Gospel. Here are some words from it broken down to their original meaning:

- *PERSUADE* is a verb meaning "to convince, by argument of true or false, or to rely."
- *PLEASE* means "the idea of exciting emotion, to be agreeable."
- *SERVANT* means "a slave, literal or figuratively, voluntary or involuntary."

If we think about this in the context of what the Word says about witnessing to others, do we try to convince people through an argument about what the Word says? Is our focus on exciting an emotion in men to agree with us? Do we even leave room to be found wrong? Or do we push our way through to be considered right?

Paul went on to say, *"If I yet pleased men, I should not be the servant of Christ."* Do you spend your life and time pleasing others or being worried about what others think or say? You can't serve God and people. You will be obedient to one of the two voices. Who do you serve?

Ask Yourself

- Am I more worried about making and keeping friends than about what God says?
- When God tells me to do something, is my first thought God-centered or people-centered?
- What is my motive for my decisions?
- Do I make my motive appear to be God when people are looking when DEEP DOWN, people are my motive?

_____

_____

_____

_____

Ask God to show you your true motive. Pray that He will show you whose voice you seek to please— whether it is God's voice or the voice of people.

❦ DAY 15 ❧

What Is My Yeast?

Today, I am thankful for: _____

_____

_____

Today's Scripture Reading Is Galatians 5:9

A little leaven [a slight inclination to error or a few false teachers] leavens the whole batch [it perverts the concept of faith and misleads the whole church].   AMP

Metaphorically, *leaven* speaks of "mental or moral corruption that can be viewed in a tendency to infect others." In the physical, a little yeast causes the whole dough to rise. In the same way, a little compromise or one wrong friend can cause emotions and other old habits to start to rise in us. When we get saved and are born again, we are made new in Christ, but sometimes a little leaven can cause the old man to resurface.

One wrong person can cause an infection in the church or among your friends, your family or even your children. Take some time and think about what your friends are pouring into you. First Corinthians 6:12 says, *"Everything is permissible for me,* but not all things are beneficial. Everything is permissible for me, but I will not be enslaved by anything [and brought under its power, allowing it to control me]" (AMP). Certain things may not be sin, but they could be a door that will lead you in that direction over time.

Complacency is an example of what can lead you into compromise. When we become complacent, we no longer have a burning desire to grow in the Lord. In Revelation 3:15-16, the Lord said, *"I know your deeds, that you are neither cold (invigorating, refreshing) nor hot (healing, therapeutic); I wish that you we were cold or hot. So, because you are lukewarm (spiritually useless), and neither hot nor cold, I will vomit you out of My mouth [rejecting you with disgust]"* (AMP).

Ask Yourself

- Is there any leaven or compromise in my daily physical life?
- Is there a little compromise in my spiritual life?
- Is there a little compromise in my thought life?

_____

_____

_____

_____

_____

Ask God to show you where any source of compromise is coming from. Ask Him how to get it out of your life without having the whole batch (your family, church or friends) infected.

✍ DAY 16 ✍

Do I Feed the Flesh or the Spirit?

Today, I am thankful for: _____

_____

_____

Today's Scripture Reading Is Galatians 5:16

But I say, walk habitually in the [Holy] Spirit [seek Him and be responsive to His guidance], and then you will certainly not carry out the desire of the sinful nature [which responds impulsively without regard for God and his precepts]. AMP

The next verse goes on to describe that the desire of the spirit is the opposite of the desire of the flesh. Before you can crucify the flesh, you must first walk with the Holy Spirit. If you are not doing this, you may not even realize when the flesh is screaming for your attention.

Our nature is self-pleasing. My feelings may be satisfied at the moment, but it's a temporary satisfaction. Ask yourself what controls you. Do physical contentment or emotions drive your decisions or do you control what you do? This scripture says that if you feed the spirit daily, you will not fulfill the desires of the sinful nature.

What are the desires of your sinful nature? Verse 19 says, *"Now the practices of the sinful nature are clearly evident: they are sexual immorality, impurity, sensuality (total irresponsibility, lack of self-control), idolatry, sorcery, hostility, strife, jealousy, fits of anger, disputes, dissensions, factions [that promote heresies], envy, drunkenness, riotous behavior and other things like these"* (AMP). Whichever you feed — spirit or flesh — will be the one that grows stronger. Which one do you feed?

Ask Yourself

- Do I feed my spirit with things that drain me or fill me?
- In the physical, do I eat what I want when I want it, or do I limit myself?
- Do I play on my phone or social media DAILY, feeding my flesh, or do I get in the Word and feed my spirit?
- When I have down time or want background noise, do I put on worship music or a TV sitcom?

_____

_____

_____

_____

Take time to ask God to show you how to overcome your fleshly desires. Pray that your spirit will become stronger than your flesh.

∽ DAY 17 ∾

Am I Fair or Unfair?

Today, I am thankful for: _____

_____

_____

Today's Scripture Reading Is
Deuteronomy 25:1-19

This chapter lists several varied laws and tells how the people of Israel were to go about things correctly. I want to focus on verses 13 through 16 for a moment:

You shall not have in your bag inaccurate weights, a heavy and a light [so you can cheat others]. You shall not have in your house inaccurate measures, a large and a small. You shall have a perfect (full) and just weight, and a perfect and just measure, SO THAT your days may be long in the land which the LORD your God gives you. For everyone who does such things, everyone who acts unjustly [without integrity] is utterly repulsive to the LORD your God.   AMP

WOW! This is intense. Are you fair or unfair? How do things that affect you and your family determine how you respond? Are you like a chameleon, changing colors every time you are around different people? We are told not to carry around different weights and measures.

Jesus said, *"For with what judgment ye judge, ye shall be judged: and with what measure ye mete, it shall be measured to you again"* (Matthew 7:2). Do you carry two different weights or measures in your bag, the one being seen outwardly by people outside of your home and the other what you are behind closed doors? We are called to be the same everywhere we go. The words *"SO THAT"* in verse 15 mean that living long days in the land God gives me is based on living with perfect and just weights and measures.

Ask Yourself

- Am I living two different lifestyles at once: The life people at church or on social media see, where life is great and going well, and the other life at home, where I am stressed and there is tension and fighting in my marriage?
- Do I paint a pretty picture on the outside that God would look at and say was hypocritical?
- Do I judge other people based on their actions, then judge myself based on my intentions (thus judging unjustly)?

_____

_____

_____

_____

Ask God to help you in the areas where your weights and measures are not just and perfect.

☙ **DAY 18** ☙

Who Am I Mentoring?

Today, I am thankful for: _____

_____

_____

Today's Scripture Reading Is Judges 1:1-36

Before he died, Moses informed the people that he would not be going with them into the Promised Land. God had designated Joshua to take them in. Then Moses laid his hands on Joshua, and Joshua took over.

Fortunately, Joshua had been mentored by Moses on how to be a leader, and there is a call on each of our lives today to teach our children and others around us how to obey God's Word and live as a leader should.

Sadly, when Joshua himself died, he hadn't mentored anyone to take his place. *"Now after the death of Joshua it came to pass, that the children of Israel asked the LORD, saying, Who shall go up for us against the Canaanites first, to fight against them? And the LORD said, Judah shall go up: behold, I have delivered the land into his hand"* (verses 1 and 2).

But look at verse 3. Judah asked Simeon to go with him to the fight to drive out the Canaanites so that they could inhabit the land. No one felt capable of doing it.

Joshua hadn't mentored anyone to take his place, so everyone had leaned on him, and when he was gone, they had no one to hold them accountable. The result was that, with twelve consecutive judges, every time one of them died, the younger generations fell back into captivity. They didn't know God as Moses and Joshua had.

Proverbs 22:6 teaches us, *"Train up a child in the way he should go: and when he is old, he will not depart from it."* This is both a promise and a warning. It's a promise, if you raise your children right, a warning if you don't. How are you doing?

Ask Yourself

- Am I mentoring my children or friends to live godly lives?
- Am I mentoring them to take a stand for what is right? Or will they sit passively by and tolerate sin?
- Am I mentoring them on how to be a leader when they have their own family?
- Am I mentoring them to build others up as they are being built up?

_____
_____
_____
_____

Ask God to show you how to teach and lead your offspring and others around you into the faith. Ask Him who you should start mentoring today and how.

✄ DAY 19 ☌

What Am I Teaching My Children?

Today, I am thankful for: _____

_____

_____

Today's Scripture Reading Is Judges 2:1-23

Chapters 1 and 2 serve as a sort of overview for the whole book of Judges and why God had to raise up judges in the first place. The first chapter shows that no one was mentored to take Joshua's place. Chapter 2 reinforces the promise from Proverbs mentioned in yesterday's devotional.

After Joshua and his generation died, the next generation didn't know God in the same heart-to-heart relationship. Verse 10 refers to the older generation (Joshua's generation) dying off and the newer generations coming up that didn't know God or the works He had done for His people.

Verse 16 goes on to say that God would raise up judges to deliver the people out of their captivity, but verse 19 is scary! It shows that after the judges God raised up had died, the people returned to their sin and corrupted themselves more than their fathers.

In situations like this, the promise of Proverbs 22:6 becomes a warning. If any generation is raised up not knowing God, when no one is there to hold them accountable, they will rebel against Him.

What lifestyle does your child see you living? Do they hear you telling stories about what God has delivered you from? Do they see a REAL GOD at work or just a FAIRY TALE?

Ask Yourself

- Am I teaching my children to hear God and fear Him?
- Am I teaching them to be obedient to what God has said?
- Am I perhaps teaching them to be followers of my opinion and to be dependent upon me instead of God?
- When they eventually leave home, what type of person will they be?
- Do the other people I come in contact with daily know God and His works?

_____

_____

_____

_____

Ask God to show you how and where you need to teach and lead those around you. Ask Him to open your eyes so that you can spiritually see what exactly you are teaching others—good or bad.

❧ DAY 20 ❧

Am I Learning Warfare?

Today, I am thankful for: _____

_____

_____

Today's Scripture Reading Is Judges 3:1-8

God left nations of hostile people in the Promised Land to teach the Israelites through war. In the past few days, we have mentioned that no one mentored or trained the next generations, so God had to train them Himself. Even if you were not raised in a godly home or taught spiritual warfare, God Himself can teach you! He left these people there to teach the Israelites something they knew nothing about (see verse 2).

In verse 4, we read that God wanted to see if the younger generations would heed His commandments. They and their parents had not driven out the pagan inhabitants of the land as they were supposed to. Instead, they intermarried with them and began to serve their false gods. These compromises began to infect the newer generations, and they didn't even realize it. Because they did evil in God's sight, He sold them into bondage for eight years.

Now God put them in a place where they would have to cry out to Him. He wanted to give them a heart revelation of who He was and what He was capable of. We cannot afford to pick a fight or even say we will win a spiritual war if we aren't obedient to God's voice. He brought these people though some training, so that they could be victorious and live in the Promised Land.

Your training ground and your battle is where you have potential to be strengthened.

Ask Yourself

- What obstacle is in my face that I need to look at as a training ground and what does God want me to learn from it?
- What area am I struggling with?
- What area of my heart is being trained?
- In what area do I need to go from head knowledge to heart knowledge?

_____

_____

_____

_____

_____

Ask God to strengthen you and show you what you are fighting and why. Start listening to and obeying His voice over the voices of fear and distrust.

DAY 21

Am I Teachable?

Today, I am thankful for: _____

_____

_____

Today's Scripture Reading Is
Judges 13:1-25

As we read about the birth of the last judge, Samson, I want us to focus on a few important details. The chapter begins with Israel sinning and doing evil in God's sight, causing her people to be bound by the Philistines for forty years. An Israelite woman, who was barren (the wife of Manoah) was visited by an angel and told that she would have a son. Because of the high calling on her son's life, there were certain guidelines she would have to live by, and there were certain guidelines she was to instill in him as well (see verses 3-5).

The woman ran to tell her husband what had happened, and he responded immediately with prayer, asking God for the angel to return. He asked God to have the angel teach them what needed to be done with the child who was to be born. God did send the angel again, and the angel told them what guidelines they and the child were to follow.

God is the ultimate Teacher. Manoah prayed for a mentor before the child was even born, for he wanted to be taught what to do. He wanted to know how to raise this son up to fulfill God's call on his life. We can learn so much from Manoah's actions. Do we even consider that *our* actions will affect how our children walk in their calling? Your lifestyle DIRECTLY affects all those around you. And the only One who knows what needs to be done so that your child can reach his or her potential is God Himself!

Ask Yourself

- Have I ever prayed for God to send someone to mentor and teach me in areas I don't yet understand?
- Am I willing to be like Manoah's wife and live by a higher standard than others around me?
- What guidelines are God speaking to me right now that I need to start implementing, to set an atmosphere for Him to move in my life?
- In what areas am I not implementing the standard that God is calling me to, so that He can release a deeper anointing upon me?

_____

_____

_____

Ask God to show you how to raise a standard in your life that will allow Him to start moving in ways He has not moved until now. Then ask Him to show you how to set guidelines in place to nurture the calling of those around you.

✒ **DAY 22** ✒

Do I Pray for Restoration?

Today, I am thankful for: _____

_____

_____

Today's Scripture Reading Is Judges 16:1-31

As Samson's story progressed, he fell in love with Delilah, a Philistine woman. The lords of the Philistines learned of this and subsequently enticed Delilah with silver to find the source of his strength. Unfortunately, Delilah fell right into the enemy's plan. Verse 16 says, *"And it came to pass, when she pressed him daily with her words, and urged him, so that his soul was vexed unto death ... ."* After enough attempts, Samson gave in and told Delilah the true source of his strength. In the end, the Philistines shaved his head, and he lost the supernatural strength he had because shaving his head was against the guidelines God had given for his life. He was then captured and put into prison. Through the course of time, Samson's hair grew out, he prayed to God, and his strength was restored to him.

Maybe you find yourself in a similar position. Were you once living a life with standards and convictions but have strayed from that life. You may have lost the victory you once had and may have been pressed by the enemy daily for so long that you gave in, not seeing how it could hurt you. It was only later that you found yourself stuck. Maybe you now have regrets and would like to return to God's favor.

Maybe, like Samson, you have been accustomed to using and relying on your own strength instead of God's. If so, it's time to turn your eyes back to Jesus today, as the Source of your strength.

Ask Yourself

- What caused me to give in to the mental battle and surrender? (Make a list of regrets or things you hold against yourself and present it to God.)
- Are there areas of my life where I lean on my own strength instead of God's?
- Are there areas of my life where I need God to miraculously restore me?

_____

_____

_____

_____

_____

Take some time and surrender your heart, even the really hard and painful parts, back to God. Give Him back the rightful place of your strength. Ask Him to show you how to forgive yourself and move on and be restored.

☙ DAY 23 ☙

What Picture Does My Life Reveal?

Today, I am thankful for: _____

_____

_____

Today's Scripture Reading Is Hosea 1:1-3

The beginning of the Word of the LORD by Hosea. And the LORD said to Hosea, Go, take unto thee a wife of whoredoms and children of whoredoms: for the land hath committed great whoredom, departing from the LORD.

Verse 2

WOW! Look at what God asked Hosea to do. He wanted Hosea's life to be a picture of what people were doing to Him. The next verse says that Hosea *"went and took Gomer,"* a harlot, to be his wife. Think about that! Hosea's life was to be an object lesson, one that we will break down over the next few days.

Hosea knew that he was to marry a prostitute, a wife who would be unfaithful to him and have children by other men.

Yet, he chose to be obedient. He was willing to be vulnerable and become an example of God's unconditional love.

God wanted to show the Israelites, through reality, what they were doing to Him in the spirit realm. Hosea's life was a picture of the spiritual relationship between the Israelites and their God. What is God trying to show me about my relationship with Him through my reality?

Ask Yourself

- What picture do people see when they look at my life?
- Do they see a merciful God?
- Do they see a harsh and judgmental God?
- Do they see a God of promises and hope?
- Do they see a God who gives up on people?
- Do they see my hurts and trials turned to victories, revealing to them a REAL God?
- Do they see my commitment to God?
- Am I willing to look at my reality and my relationship with God and see if they line up?

_____

_____

_____

_____

_____

_____

Pray that through your reality you would see what you do to God spiritually. Pray for your eyes to be opened in the next few days as we dive into what spiritual idolatry is all about.

❧ DAY 24 ❧

Does My Battle Bring Me To God?

Today, I am thankful for: _____

_____

_____

Today's Scripture Reading Is Hosea 2:1-13 and Romans 8:28

This chapter of Hosea starts by showing the idolatry of Israel. God said, in verse 6, *"therefore, behold* [because of the idolatry of verse five], *I will hedge thy way with thorns, and make a wall, that she shall not find her paths."* When I choose to put idols above God, I find myself in a battle that I cannot escape. I may even find myself in a battle with demons. How can I fight things like fear, anxiety or depression? How can I get myself out of this battle?

I love what verse 7 says: *"THEN shall she say, I will go and return to my first husband; for then was it better with me than now."* Who was the first husband? It was God. When our struggle with demons becomes intense, we often realize we cannot keep doing things on our own. In this way, the struggle sends me back to God. The Word of God states that what Satan has meant for evil, God can turn to my good. The struggle Satan wants me to stay bound in and not get free actually sends me to God for my freedom!

Verse 8 shows that God sees past our idolatry. Israel did not know God was her Source of provision and increase, and she gave that title to Baal. We don't realize that our strength and abilities are given by God. We can get to the place where we consider a job or our increase in knowledge or skill to have come through our ability and not God's and we are blind to it at the time.

Now, in verse 11 through 13, God allowed Israel to hit rock bottom. Everything she thought she had was taken away. But look at verse 13, *"I will visit upon her the days of Baalim, wherin she burned incense to them."* God was visiting her to the very place that had caused her to run to idolatry. Why? God wanted to restore her. He wanted the idolatry to stop and wanted her to surrender her whole heart to Him. Tomorrow we will go into her restoration.

Take a moment to think about the battles you are in. Are you headed for rock bottom? You may be in it now. Has this ever been an experience of your past?

Ask Yourself

- What causes me to run to idols?
- What makes me think I can do things in my own strength?
- What battle am I in that I need to cry out to God for deliverance from?

_____

_____

Pray that you will see God and be able to call out to Him before you have to hit rock bottom, that you will see the struggle you're in and the idol you are serving for what it is. Don't run away from God. Run to Him!

⚈ **DAY 25** ⚈

How Intimate Am I with God?

Today, I am thankful for: _____

_____

_____

Today's Scripture Reading Is Hosea 2:14-23

While Israel was at her rock bottom, God began to lure her into the wilderness, as when she had left Egypt, and He began to speak comfortably to her. In this way, He eased His people.

In verse 16, we see them going from calling God their *"master"* to calling Him their *"husband."* WOW! The people of Israel moved from religion to relationship! They went from hearing how much God loved them to experiencing Him pulling them out from idolatry. They experienced God rescuing and restoring them. They went from "head knowledge" of God to "heart knowledge" of Him! They now had the intimacy of God as being their husband, rather than being slaves under His mastery.

All the people had known in Egypt was slavery. so they had exhibited a slave mindset with God. He had to renew their minds, so that they could experience the intimacy He desired with them. Because of the relationship they now had with their Creator, Heaven and Earth now lined up, and God would sow them back into the land.

Once you get heart knowledge in an area of your relationship with God, He will sow you back to be a witness to others around you. You then start to reproduce yourself in others. Through your own intimacy with God, you have the ability to help others reach out to Him and gain the intimacy He desires with them!

Ask Yourself

- What part of God do I live in head knowledge or heart knowledge? Is it in mercy? Forgiveness? Love? Grace?
- Am I willing to be honest with myself about why I run to other things instead of God?
- When I am stressed out about finances, children, etc., do I run to TV, social media, friends, gossip, food or drugs to vent or gain comfort?
- Am I now free enough to ask God to show me how to reproduce myself, to start becoming fruitful where He leads me?

_____

_____

_____

Thank God for the heart knowledge you received when you were honest with yourself and with Him. Ask Him to help you see what's really going on and why you sometimes run from Him.

✂ **DAY 26** ✍

Am I Married To Christ?

Today, I am thankful for: _____

_____

_____

Today's Scripture Reading Is Hosea 3:1-5

Spend some time focusing on verses 1 and 4. Here Hosea's marriage is paralleled with Israel's idolatry against God. Even though Gomer was a prostitute and would go after other men, God wanted Hosea to pursue her anyway. This was a picture of God's unconditional love for you and me! Hosea told Gomer, *"Thou shalt not play the harlot, and thou shalt not be for another man"* (verse 3), and God says the SAME THING to us in verse 4. He wants us to go *"many days without."* In other words, He wants us to have a lifestyle change.

When we got saved, we entered into a marriage with Christ. Let me ask you: Have you been faithful to Him? In the natural, we don't get married and then only see our spouse twice a week. We spend every day with him or her. We talk with him or her. We want to know how their day has gone. We want to know we were missed and thought of. And God is the same. We do these things in the physical, but what is our spiritual life like? Do we only see Christ or spend time with Him on the days we attend church services?

When we get married in the physical, it is a total lifestyle change. We women change our name and our address. We become one with our spouse, and we are now in a relationship, partnered one to the other. Is there anything in the physical that reveals your marriage to Christ?

Ask Yourself

- Do I spend time with God DAILY?
- Do I meditate upon Him and talk with Him?
- Do I ask His opinion about whether or not I should get involved in something I may want to do?
- Do I think He misses me and wants to spend more time with me?
- If not, why?

_____

_____

_____

_____

_____

Pray that you will be able to be faithful to God in your marriage relationship with Him.

✍ DAY 27 ✍

Am I Unfaithful To God?

Today, I am thankful for: _____

_____

_____

Today's Scripture Reading Is
Hosea 4:1-19

In this chapter of Hosea, God brought a charge of disobedience against Israel in the physical and in the spiritual. Physically, God told them there was no truth, no mercy, and no knowledge of God in the land. They swore, lied, killed, stole, committed adultery and fought. Spiritually, they were committing idolatry. Verse 18 says, *"They habitually go to play the prostitute"* (AMP). The KJV uses *continually,* but the meaning is the same. God was telling them that they were unfaithful to Him out of habit! What does that mean? It might refer to some everyday task we do that we don't involve Him in. In my heart, for instance, am I being the provider instead of God? Do I lean on my own strength and ability or that of a spouse or a company and not God?

The people of Hosea's day would find it easy to condemn Gomer for adultery, because they could see her actions. But I'm sure they weren't happy when their own secret lives were exposed. Are you quick to judge others by their actions because you can see them? Do you assume you know their motives? What do *you* do out of habit?

Typically, for instance, we pray over our meals (out of habit), but is your heart really in your prayer? Are you acting more out of a religious habit rather than a relationship? No one wants their spouse to do things for them out of mere obligation or just to make themselves look good. We want their actions to be sincere. Are your actions from your heart and sincere with God?

Ask Yourself

- What are my religious habits?
- Is God just a habit with me?
- Do my habits lead me *to* God or *away from* Him?
- Am I in a religion or in a true relationship?

_____

_____

_____

_____

_____

_____

_____

_____

_____

Ask God to open your eyes to the motives behind what you do and why you do it. Ask Him to show you areas where He doesn't have your whole heart.

℘ DAY 28 ℘

Do I Have a Religion Or a Relationship?

Today, I am thankful for: _____

_____

_____

Today's Scripture Reading Is Hosea 6:1-11

In the first two verses, Israel repented:

> *Come, and let us return unto the LORD: for he hath torn, and he will heal us; he hath smitten, and he will bind us up. After two days will he revive us: in the third day he will raises us up, and we shall live in his sight.*

They repented, thinking that God's wrath would only endure a few days, but God responded to them:

> *For your goodness is as a morning cloud, and as the early dew it goeth away.*   Verse 4

A morning cloud is the morning dew. As soon as the sun rises and heats up, the dew evaporates and is gone. There is no substance to morning dew. It dissipates QUICKLY with the sun and its heat.

Let me ask you a question: When you repent and start to do right by the Lord, would God say it is "as the morning dew?"

When you are tired and a time of pressure comes, do you go back to your old ways? Look at what God says in verse 6:

For I desired mercy, and not sacrifice; and the knowledge of God more than burnt offerings.

God wants our heart in a relationship, not a religion. A religion will not withstand the heat of the day, but a relationship will! In verse 7, God said:

But they like men have transgressed the covenant: there have they dealt treacherously against me.

Treacherously means "offensively." How about you?

Ask Yourself

• Does God have my heart in a relationship or am I just in a religion?
• Is my goodness to God like the morning dew that evaporates or does it last through the heat of a pressured time?
• Am I repenting because of His wrath or do I truly mean it when I return to God?
• If I'm just repenting to escape His wrath, would God tell me that I am offending Him?

_____
_____
_____
_____
_____
_____

Ask God to show you if your goodness is like the morning dew or if it will last through the heat of pressure.

✍ **DAY 29** ✍

Do I Deal with My Emotions?

Today, I am thankful for: _____

_____

_____

Today's Scripture Reading Is Hosea 7:6-7

For they have made ready their heart like an oven, whiles they lie in wait: their baker sleepeth all the night; in the morning it burneth as a flaming fire. They are all hot as an oven, and have devoured their judges; all their kings are fallen: there is none among them that calleth unto me.

They made their heart like an oven? They allowed things to sit, simmer and get heated. How many times do we allow our thoughts and emotions to dwell into the night, getting us all worked up, while we sit and simmer on the situation with what-if scenarios?

They slept, but in the morning, their hearts burned like a flaming fire. If we don't deal with an issue the day it comes up, we suppress our emotions and allow that thing to grow bigger the next day. Suppressing your emotions will only cause matters to accelerate! Ephesians 4:26-27 tells us *"Be ye angry, and sin not: let not the sun go down upon your wrath: neither give place to the devil."*

Hosea explained why his emotions got to this point. *Wrath* in this verse means "anger," but it could be any emotion. Jesus got angry and flipped tables. Anger, in itself, is not a bad thing. It's what you do with your emotions that could lead to sin. God wants us to deal with our situations. If we don't, we may heed the voice of our emotions and not call out to God. When we sit and let things fester or allow our emotions to get the best of us, we react impulsively.

Ask Yourself

- When my emotions are screaming at me, do I get wise counsel or do I just react?
- Do I do whatever gives me temporary satisfaction in the moment or do I seek God for what truly needs to be done?
- Do I let the sun go down on my wrath, only to wake up on the wrong side of the bed the next morning and have a worse situation?

_____

_____

_____

_____

_____

Ask God what is happening in your life. Do you need to learn to deal with your emotions, rather than suppressing them?

⚡ DAY 30 ⚡

What Is Judgement?

Today, I am thankful for: _____

_____

_____

Today's Scripture Reading Is
Zephaniah 2:1-15

The end of this chapter records judgment on the nations that performed wickedness. God always provides an open door, and He saves the remnant that "chooses" the open door and follows Him as children.

The chapter begins by stating, *"Gather yourselves together ... before the day of the LORD's anger come upon you"* (verses 1-2). *"Seek ye the LORD, ... seek righteousness, seek meekness"* (verse 3). We hear the word *repent,* and we assume that it refers to sin. While that may be true for us, God also repented, and this may catch you by surprise. You may wonder, how could God repent, if He never sins? *Repent* simply means "to turn, to go in the opposite direction."

Challenge yourself by finding where and why God repented. Seek to truly understand the term *repent,* which we use very lightly at times.

We are also to seek righteousness, meaning that we are to seek to do what's right. We are to do what the Word of God says. We are to seek meekness and humility, which is a quiet spirit. If you do this, there is a possibility that you will be hid in the day of the Lord's anger (see verse 3)!

So, the road we are to travel on is:

- To repent and seek God
- To obey God and seek righteousness
- To humble ourselves by seeking meekness

The opposite of humility is arrogance and pride. In verse 10, God said that their punishment would come because of pride.

Ask Yourself

- In this season of my life, what is God asking me to do?
- Am I obedient?
- Do I need to repent and turn back to God and obey what He is telling me?

_____

_____

_____

_____

_____

Ask God to show you how to seek true humility and not a false humility, as you endeavor to live your life for Him.

Do I See the Whole Picture?

Today, I am thankful for: _____

_____

_____

Today's Scripture Reading Is
Habakkuk 1:1-11

Have you ever found yourself crying out to God and asking Him:

- Why is this happening?
- Will You ever defend me?
- What is going on?
- How can You let this person get away with this?
- Why didn't You stop them from being influenced?

That's what happened in the beginning of this chapter. Habakkuk was crying out for the people around him, and God's answer was simple and yet profound. He said, *"I will work a work in your days, which ye will not believe, though it be told to you"* (verse 5). While we see hurt and confusion, see the reality that we live in, see the people around us, God sees behind the scenes! We see chaos, while God is both stirring things up and settling the scene.

Think of a chess game. You may have to lose a few pieces to set up a checkmate. God can do a checkmate without ever losing any pieces. We just don't see the whole picture.

God went on to say that He was raising the people up and setting the stage for checkmate. He will always have the final say, and, in the end, we will win.

Ask Yourself

- Do I jump in to vindicate myself and fix a situation, while still seeing only part of the picture?
- Do I sit back and trust that God's hand is in the middle of my situation and that His timing is better than mine?

_____

_____

_____

_____

_____

_____

_____

_____

_____

Ask God to show you the situation or the person from "His" perspective. Start to trust Him in every area of your life, especially when you are going through a storm.

✂ **DAY 32** ꙮ

What Is the Fruit I'm Producing?

Today, I am thankful for: _____

_____

_____

Today's Scripture Reading Is Isaiah 5:1-4 and Galatians 5:16-26

We are God's vine and, therefore, should bear fruit. These verses detail what God does to help the vine produce good fruit, and they also describe what He does when the vine doesn't bear. God has done everything He could for the vineyard He planted, and when He looks at it, He expects to find good grapes. Instead, He finds WILD GRAPES. *Grapes* here could be translated as "to bear fruit." *Wild grapes* could be translated as "worthless things, stink berries, stench or foul odor." They may even be "poison berries." Galatians lists the fruits of the flesh and fruits of the spirit. The fruits of the flesh are these (see Galatians 5:19-21):

- Adultery
- Uncleanness
- Idolatry
- Hatred
- Emulations
- Strife

- Fornication
- Lasciviousness
- Witchcraft
- Variance
- Wrath
- Seditions

- Heresies
- Murders
- Reveling
- Envying
- Drunkenness

The fruits of the Spirit are these (see Galatians 5:22-23):

- Love   - Joy   - Peace
- Longsuffering   - Gentleness   - Goodness
- Faith   - Meekness   - Temperance

If you don't know what some of these words mean, take the time to look them up. Then circle the words from both lists that you see manifesting in your own personal life.

Look at the fruit of your life that you have circled and know that this is what you may be feeding others. The people you influence eat the fruit you produce.

Ask Yourself:

- Would God look at me and say that I have produced good fruit or wild grapes and why?

_____

_____

_____

_____

_____

_____

_____

Pray that God would show you how to produce good fruit in your daily life.

❧ DAY 33 ❧

Am I Disobedient by Choice?

Today, I am thankful for: _____

_____

_____

Today's Scripture Reading Is
Isaiah 7:10-12

God told Ahaz to ask for a sign, but Ahaz had an excuse as to why he wouldn't do it. In verse 12, he said, *"I will not ask, neither will I tempt the LORD."* God went on to tell Ahaz that it was one thing to weary men, but he should not weary God. Then God told him about the sign He intended to give him.

There are various possibilities as to why Ahaz didn't want to ask for this sign, but his reasoning doesn't matter. It was an act of disobedience. It is possible that Ahaz didn't understand what he was being asked to do, and it is also possible that he didn't want to hear what God wanted to tell him.

Don't we all sometimes act in a similar way when God asks us to do something we don't want to do? Doesn't He ask us to express how we feel in a certain area, but we give a religious excuse to justify why we are unwilling to obey? Excuses or not, isn't it disobedience to *not* do what God tells us to do?

If someone asks you to help with an outreach or ministry at church, do you respond, "I'll pray about it and get back with you?" Do you actually pray about it? Most don't. But why wouldn't we? Perhaps because we know that if we pray and God says, "Yes, go do it," and we don't obey, we are being disobedient. So, to make ourselves feel better, we don't even pray about it. That way, we don't feel guilty for not having obeyed God.

Ask Yourself:

- In what area or areas do I have a religious answer or excuse to justify myself? This may make me look good on the outside to others, but on the inside I know that it's nothing more than a feeble excuse.

_____

_____

_____

_____

_____

_____

_____

_____

Pray that God would help you to be true to yourself and obedient to Him. Pray that He opens your eyes to the area or areas of your life in which you are disobedient and don't even realize it.

✄ DAY 34 ℘

Do I Pray Before Acting?

Today, I am thankful for: _____

_____

_____

Today's Scripture Reading Is
Isaiah 8:19-22 and Psalm 25:4-5

In this section of Isaiah, the people were seeking familiar spirits, wizards and false gods for answers. Verse 21 says, *"And it shall come to pass, that when they shall be hungry, they shall fret themselves, and curse their king and their god and look upward."* They were making their own plans, and then, when they got hungry, they cursed their gods and their king.

Do I put God in the middle of my decision making? Do I blame Him for things that go wrong around me ... when I haven't even asked Him about it before I acted? Does God get the blame for some of my self-induced problems? If so, I need to pray for God's plan and His blessings on that plan, rather than asking Him to bless *my* plan. I should pray first and then make a plan, not make a plan and then pray!

Psalm 25:4-5, part of one of David's psalms, says, *"Shew me thy ways, O Lord; teach me thy paths. Lead me in thy truth and teach me: for thou art the God of my salvation; on thee do I wait all the day."* David had the attitude of waiting, even all day, on God's leading and teaching.

What attitude do you have? Do you seek everything under the sun, until you get the answer you want, then, when it doesn't work out, get mad and blame God or others? Or do you have David's attitude and say, "I will wait on You, Lord?"

Ask Yourself

- Where in my life have I acted on my own plan and then prayed for God to bless what I had done?
- Where do I need more of David's heart of waiting on God at all costs and letting God answer me?

_____

_____

_____

_____

_____

_____

_____

Ask God to help you develop a lifestyle of going to Him in prayer for everything and then heeding His voice. Praying first and then acting puts God fully in charge of the process.

❧ DAY 35 ❧

Do I Judge Others?

Today, I am thankful for: _____

_____

_____

Today's Scripture Reading Is
Isaiah 11:1-5, John 7:24
and 1 Samuel 16:6-12

Isaiah 11 is a foretelling of the coming of Jesus, the Branch out of Jesse. It says that the Spirit would rest upon Him and He would judge righteously. Verse 3 states, *"And he will not judge after the sight of his eyes, neither reprove after the hearing of his ears."* Verse 2 spoke of the Spirit that would empower Him. That Spirit would make Him *"of quick understanding"* and would help Him not to judge by what He saw with His natural eyes or heard with His natural ears. It is easy not to be led by the Holy Spirit and, rather, to judge by what you see or hear. You must be Spirit led to be able to see past the physical perspective and to see the spiritual influence.

We can see why people do what they do, but John 7:24 states, *"Judge not according to the appearance, but judge righteous judgment."* That is God's ideal for us.

Read the passage from 1 Samuel and think about what the prophet was feeling as he went forth to anoint a king to succeed Saul. He was looking at those handsome sons walking up to him and saying to himself, "This one has to be the one God will choose." But each time, God said no. He then told the prophet, *"For man looketh on the outward appearance, but the LORD looketh on the heart."*

Ask Yourself

- Do I judge people's heart at times, assuming that I know what they mean and how they mean it?
- Do I judge their motives without knowing them?
- Do I judge by appearance, body language or perhaps just the tone of their voice?
- It's extremely easy to judge others, but do I look at and judge myself by the same standards I use to judge others?
- Where have I judged others by their actions and then judged myself by my intentions?

_____

_____

_____

_____

_____

Pray for God to show you areas in which you are judging by what you see and hear. Allow Him to do the judging while you sit back and love on God's people.

✂ DAY 36 ✄

Why Do I Fear?

Today, I am thankful for: _____

_____

_____

Today's Scripture Reading Is Isaiah 12:2, Exodus 15:2 and Psalm 118:14

All three of these passages say the same thing, nearly word for word. Notice that, in the King James Version of Isaiah, there is a colon after the word *afraid*. It means that the words following the colon describe what is in front of the colon. In other words, you can ONLY trust God and not fear if He is your strength and song.

The words *salvation* here can also be translated as "deliverance." *Song* could be translated as "music or melody." We know that the walls of Jericho fell on the seventh day when the horns blew. Music is a form of spiritual warfare. It always was and always will be. With that in mind, I can only trust God and not fear because I know that He is my strength and my song. He is the One who battles for me. He is my Vindicator! Trust comes through Him being my strength and song, and if I fear, it means that God is *not* my strength and song.

We sometimes fear because we don't know God as our strength. We battle and work in our own strength, working out of what we can see, working though our current "reality," working through what we predict will happen. We play God in our own lives because of the wounds and hurts that cause us to self-protect.

Or we can fear because we don't know God as our song. We don't see Him as our defense. We don't think that He will vindicate us. Therefore, we have to fight on our own. We do our battling physically, mentally and verbally. We strive to prove ourselves, rather than sitting under the safety and rest of His wings. I need to get off of the throne and let Him be God. Am I allowing God to work through me and for me?

Ask Yourself (in situations that cause you to fear)

- God, are You my strength in this area or am I leaning on myself?
- God, are You my song?
- Are you fighting for me, or am I fighting for myself and trying to clear my own name?

_____

_____

_____

_____

Surrender this area to God in prayer and let Him have His rightful place.

℘ DAY 37 ℚ

Do I Forget About God?

Today, I am thankful for: _____

_____

_____

Today's Scripture Reading Is
Isaiah 17:6-11

Isaiah 17 teaches us to look to God, our Maker, and have respect to the Holy One of Israel. Verse 8 states, *"And he shall not look to the altars, the work of his hands, neither shall respect that which his fingers have made, either the groves, or the images."* This refers to idols. If you look to God, you have no need for idols in your life.

Verse 10 states, *"BECAUSE thou hast forgotten the God of thy salvation, and hast not been mindful of the rock of thy strength, THEREFORE shalt thou plant pleasant plants, and shalt set it with strange slips."* This is how we construct an idol. We forget what God has done for us and begin to think we did it by our own strength.

Verse 11 shows that as idolatry grows and flourishes, *"The harvest shall be a heap in the day of grief and of desperate sorrow."* We don't even realize we have made an idol until we suddenly reap the harvest from it.

An idol starts to form when we shift our focus, forgetting the God of our salvation and not being mindful of the Rock of our strength. If

I forget why I am who I am today or how I got here, I have started the process of creating an idol. If I don't keep my focus on the fact that God has provided me with this job, it can easily shift to "because of my ability, I have the job." I become my own provider, instead of God being my Provider. I take His place on the throne of my heart in that particular area of my life.

If I am offended with God for allowing something bad to happen or not intervening when I thought He should, I may start to act on my own strength instead of following Him. I may take matters into my own hands and start to play God by trying to fix my reality. I may intervene where I think there needs to be intervention.

Someone, in every situation, gets the glory. Do I give the glory to God or do I keep some of it for myself? I may think, "It couldn't have happened without me" or "I'm glad I was there." We must remember that it is not by us but by God who ordained us to be there. If I forget to give glory to God, then I keep what belongs to Him, putting myself on the throne and creating idols and mindsets that I will then live by.

Ask Yourself

- What area or areas of my life have I not given God the glory or recognition for, and, instead, have tended to lean on my own strength?

_____

_____

_____

Turn back to God in prayer, dethroning yourself and giving Him His proper glory. Ask Him to show you where you have set up your own idols.

⚡ **DAY 38** ⚡

What Is the Importance of Heart Knowledge?

Today, I am thankful for: _____

_____

_____

Today's Scripture Reading Is
Isaiah 19:1-25

The beginning of this chapter is about Egypt, and Egypt represents slavery and bondage. If you are in Egypt, you will have idols and a hard heart (see verse 1), you will fight against other Christians (see verse 2), your worldly spirit and counsel will fail (see verse 3), you will be oppressed (see verse 4), you will battle a perverse spirit (see verse 14), and emotions of fear and terror will rise within you (see verses 16 and 17). Verse 20 says, *"For they shall cry unto the LORD because of the oppressors, and he shall send them a savior, and a great one, and he shall deliver them."*

Verse 21 declares, *"And the LORD shall be known to Egypt, and the Egyptians shall know the LORD in that day, and shall do sacrifice and oblation; yea, they shall vow a vow unto the LORD, and perform it."* It goes on to tell how God will heal Egypt.

To know is to perceive and understand. You have to get to the place in your life where you go from head knowledge of the stories you have heard to heart knowledge, an understanding of who God is.

After reading chapter 19, ask God to show you where you are in *your* life. If you don't know Him with heart knowledge, I am confident that He will show you. Ask Him to melt your heart so that you can begin to understand how to be free from the bondages of Egypt.

Ask Yourself

- Why do I have a hard heart?
- What wounds am I unwilling to let go of?
- What idols or walls do I have up that I use to protect myself from others or even God, because I don't feel as though He is there for me?
- Am I in a place where people are my enemies?
- Do I feel oppressed or weighed down?
- Am I battling a perverse spirit?
- Do I battle to keep my emotions from rising and getting the best of me?

_____

_____

_____

_____

_____

Ask God for heart knowledge of who He is and how He is now pulling you out from Egypt and into the Promised Land.

⚮ DAY 39 ⚭

Do I Learn from God's Judgements?

Today, I am thankful for: _____

_____

_____

Today's Scripture Reading Is Isaiah 26:8-10 and 1 Peter 4:17-18

These passages teach us about judgment. Isaiah said, *"For when thy judgments are in the earth, the inhabitants of the world will learn righteousness."* Peter declared that judgement must begin with the House of God. What is the purpose behind God's judgments? Believe it or not, they are for your good.

Why is it that everyone else can get away with something, but if you try it, you get caught? For example, if you were to speed down the highway, you would get a ticket. The one time you do this, you get caught. Your own disobedient action is causing you heartache.

And how is this a good thing? God's judgements are always redemptive in nature. When you get caught, that's God correcting you as a loving Father, the same type of correction you would offer to your natural child. Judgements are meant to show you the right way to live. They are here in the physical to get your attention. We are to be a godly example to the world around us, and, if we fail to do that, how, then, will others know to do better?

God's Word shows us a right and a wrong way to live in His sight. It tells us what He accepts and what He hates.

Ask Yourself

- Do I search God's Word for my own good, or do I lean on others to teach me the right way to live?
- What judgements am I currently facing that show me a better way to live?

_____

_____

_____

_____

_____

_____

_____

_____

_____

Ask God to allow you to see past the judgements you may feel now and see what, in your life, needs to be adjusted, to line up with His Word.

⚹ DAY 40 ⚹

Do I Make Peace with God?

Today, I am thankful for: _____

_____

_____

Today's Scripture Reading Is
Isaiah 27:5, Matthew 5:9 and 11:29-30

Jesus said, *"Blessed are the peacemakers: for they shall be called the children of God."* Twice in Isaiah God said, *"Make peace with me."* We are to take hold of His strength and make peace with Him, and in order to grab on to His strength, we must let go of our own.

Jeremiah 17:5 states, *"Thus saith the LORD; cursed be the man that trusteth in man, and maketh flesh his arm, and whose heart departeth from the LORD."* When we trust in ourselves, we place ourselves under a curse. If we trust in ourselves, we depart from God and must return to Him. Are you a peacemaker with God? Do you try to keep Him and yourself happy at the same time?

To let go of your own strength, you must be willing to be vulnerable. You must trust God in the area of your heart where you are hurt and wounded. And it can be very scary to open up wounds to God and allow His healing to come in. What would stop you from trusting God with the vulnerable areas of *your* heart?

Are you in offense toward God and, maybe, don't even realize it? Could it be possible that you are offended at God because He allowed something to happen, causing you to feel unprotected or unloved? If so, now you have a wall between you and God because you think He won't protect you. Are you trying to protect yourself? God is saying that we must expose our offenses. We must bring our hurts into the light, allowing the healing and freedom that come from making things right with Him to begin in us.

Ask Yourself

- What do I need to make right with God?
- Where do I feel like I work in my own strength instead of in His strength?
- Where do I need to make peace with God?

Ask God about the area or areas of your life where you are working in your own strength. Then release those things to God and allow Him to heal you. Let Him be your Strength today.

⚡ DAY 41 ⚡

What Is Discernment?

Today, I am thankful for: _____

_____

_____

Today's Scripture Reading Is Isaiah 28:23-29

The passage begins with, *"Give ye ear, ... hear my voice; hearken, ... hear my speech."* For God to say to us, "Stop and listen to Me" tells us that we may be listening to someone else. Too often we heed another voice.

God went on to use a parable about a farmer plowing and planting and instructed the farmer which tools to use, so as not to destroy the fruit during harvest. What is the harvest today? It is a harvest of ripe souls to be brought into God's Kingdom. How do we bring in that harvest? By heeding God's voice.

Jeremiah 4:3 said, *"Break up your fallow ground, and sow not among thorns."* This is referring to the ground of our hearts. God knows the wounds and hurts that have occurred in our lives, hardening our hearts. He knows what needs to take place to soften our hearts. He knows what words need to be said and when the right timing is for those words. What are we planting for those around us? Hope? Encouragement? Faith? Defeat? Stress? Disbelief? Abandonment?

Verses 27-28 refer to some fruit being tender so that you can bruise or break that fruit. The wisdom of plowing, planting, and harvesting comes from God! This parable lays out an order in which we plow, plant and harvest. There is a time for:

- **Working the ground** (verse 24), opening and softening the heart so that people can receive what God wants them to hear.
- **Planting:** When the ground is level, then plant (verse 25). When God says speak, then speak. Wait on Him. Don't just talk to be talking and filling the air.
- **Using Tools:** Certain tools are used for harvest (verse 27). This refers to different approaches to different people. There is no one-way-fixes-all approach.
- **Stopping:** If they didn't stop in time, the horses could damage the fruit (verse. 28). There is a time to stop and allow the person to heal and process what God is showing them.
- **Using Wisdom:** This wisdom is from God (verse 29) and is part of discernment. We have to be willing to be Spirit-led and not do what we think needs to be done. Remember, God knows the big picture of every life.

Ask Yourself

- Where, in this parable, do I fit?
- Where, in the time-frame for harvest, do I need to sit back and start leaning on God instead of my own strength?

_____

_____

Ask God to strengthen His discernment in you!

℘ **DAY 42** ℚ

Am I Hypocritical?

Today, I am thankful for: _____

_____

_____

Today's Scripture Reading Is Isaiah 29:13-16, Matthew 15:7-11 and Mark 7:6-13

In Isaiah 29:13, the Lord said, *"This nation approaches [Me only] with their words and honors Me [only] with their lip service, but they remove their hearts far from Me, and their reverence for Me is a tradition that is learned by rote [without any regard for its meaning]"* (AMP). You can do and say all the right things and yet keep your heart at a distance from God. Outwardly, you are doing what a Christian should be doing, but your heart isn't in it. Are you pursuing God inwardly like you were created to do?

What would stop you from pursuing God the way you were created to pursue Him? Well, the way you are taught can stop you. We are taught by our family, school, social media, TV or even society what pursuing God looks like. We are taught what respect and honor look like. We are taught to fear God, but is it the right type of fear?

Matthew 15:8-9 restates Isaiah, but then it adds the fact that such worship is *"vain."* When is our worship in vain or worthless? Our worship means nothing if it is a ritual and not from a relationship. God said that every seed will reproduce after its own kind. If we are teaching *"the commandments of men,"* that is our mindset, and then we reproduce in others what we believe. If we believe in self-protection because we have never allowed God to heal that area of our heart, then we will teach others to self-protect in the same manner.

Mark 7:13 states, *"Making the word of God of none effect THROUGH your tradition, which ye have delivered."* If we choose to stay in our carnal mindset, in our tradition (what life has taught us), then we remove the power from the Word of God in that area of our life. For example, Deuteronomy says twice that everything we put our hand to will prosper, but if I believe that the state of the economy dictates if I get a promotion or not, then that mindset will dictate my future. And it is a mindset contrary to the Word of God. If I believe that I can only prosper in a good economy, then I remove the power from the Word of God operating in this area of my life.

Ask Yourself

- What am I praying for and what do I believe about what I am praying for?

_____

_____

Prayerfully find scriptures to stand on and then change your mindset to line up with the Word of God. Change your heart and come closer to God in prayer.

℘ DAY 43 ℘

Would God Call Me Rebellious?

Today, I am thankful for: _____

_____

_____

Today's Scripture Reading Is Isaiah 30:1-3

Who do you go to for a plan of action when a situation occurs that you don't know how to handle? Through Isaiah, God spoke to the Israelites and said, *"Woe to the rebellious children, saith the LORD, that take counsel BUT NOT of me; and that cover with a covering, BUT NOT of my spirit, that they may add sin to sin"* (verse 1). God told them that they were going to Egypt without asking Him. They were strengthening themselves in the might of the Pharaoh and trusting in the shadow of Egypt! In Psalm 91:1, we are told to rest *"under the shadow of the Almighty."*

The Israelites had been freed from the slavery and bondage of Egypt, but then, as they were traveling through the wilderness, they decided they wanted to go back to Egypt because they were afraid they would die in the wilderness. Their thoughts were trying to dictate their actions.

Egypt represents what we are bound to, our survival mode. This is the area in our life that controls us. Our wounds and hurts are not healed, so we self-protect. These areas become infected and dictate our future. Walls go up, to prevent us from being hurt more. God wants to set us free!

When Isaiah said, *"that they may add sin to sin,"* he was referring to an offense or, at times, a habitual sinfulness. There are times that we get free from something (a mindset or a bondage) and do well. But then something happens that triggers old walls of self-protection. It is easy to want to return to an old comfort zone, to return to your previous form of Egypt. You want to strengthen yourself in the might of Pharaoh, which means the old lies you once believed protected you.

When we are born again, we become a new creature in Christ. Our old man dies, and should remain dead. But examples of going back to Egypt could be self-rejection (I reject myself before someone else does, so it doesn't hurt so bad when they do) or self-protection (I purposely don't make myself vulnerable to other people for fear of being taken advantage of or betrayed).

Ask Yourself

- What part of MY EGYPT do I run to "for counsel" or "to cover a hurt" instead of running to God?
- Would God look at me and say, "You are rebellious?"

_____

_____

Ask God to show you why you run to Egypt instead of to Him.

⍫ DAY 44 ⍫

What Is the Enemy's Strategic Plan? (Part 1)

Today, I am thankful for: _____

_____

_____

Today's Scripture Reading Is Isaiah 36:3-9 and 2 Kings 18:1-8

Second Kings 18 deals with the reign of Hezekiah. According to the Scriptures, King Hezekiah did everything right in God's eyes. He tore down the idols, he trusted in God like no other before him, and he followed all the commandments God had given to Moses. Because of this, God was with him, and he prospered.

King Hezekiah rebelled against the King of Assyria and refused to serve him. In Isaiah, we see the King of Assyria sending a message to Hezekiah through a man named Rabshakeh, who then went to three other men before the message reached Hezekiah. There were now four people between the two kings. The King of Assyria was trying to get Israel to surrender without a fight, and look at how he went about it:

#1). Rabshakeh questioned the three men's trust in God and made it seem like God was mad at them, because, he said, King Hezekiah had torn down God's altars instead of the altars of idols. He was planting seeds of CONFUSION in their minds by twisting what actually happened.

#2). The King of Assyria then tried to BRIBE AND MANIPULATE the men by offering them two thousand horses if they would sign a peace treaty.

#3). He then went on to plant FEAR in their minds by telling them that the King of Assyria was doing God's work and they would win if they helped him.

This is the same way Satan will come at you. He will try to make you give up without a fight. He comes #1). Through confusion and doubt, #2). Through manipulation, making it look like a good idea, and #3). through fear.

Ask Yourself

- What part of the enemy's plan am I experiencing right now? Confusion? Manipulation? Fear?
- Or am I experiencing all three at the same time?

_____

_____

_____

_____

Ask God to show you the truth of the situation you are facing. He is the truth, and the truth WILL set you free. Seek God for guidance and clarity as you face any situation.

ᚦ **DAY 45** ᚱ

What Is the Enemy's Strategic Plan? (Part 2)

Today, I am thankful for: _____

_____

_____

Today's Scripture Reading Is Isaiah 36:11-22

Yesterday, we read about how the enemy's plan is to get you to surrender without a fight. We could see how he inserts other people into the middle of a situation. He plants seeds of confusion, manipulation and fear. Continuing the story in Isaiah, we see that the three other men asked Rabshakeh to speak in the Syrian language (so that they could understand) and NOT to speak in the Jew's language (so that others around them would not understand). But what did Rabshakeh do? He cried in a loud voice, in the Jew's language, warning them that Hezekiah was trying to deceive them. In this way, he continued with the seed of FEAR that we saw yesterday.

Rabshakeh went on to tell all those around to act on impulse, and when we act impulsively, we act out of fear and emotion. He wanted them to make an agreement in exchange for a present. This was bribery and manipulation. Verse 16 speaks of a treaty, but there is a colon in the sentence. That colon tells us what treaty they were referring to. It was the same treaty the enemy tries to make with us. He told them that they would be able to eat EVERYONE OF HIS OWN VINE, AND HIS OWN FIG TREE, AND DRINK OF HIS OWN CISTERN, and Satan offers us this same chance to get back on our throne.

The King of Assyria was offering a counterfeit to the Promised Land, exactly as the enemy does with us today. The Promise Land was said to be flowing with milk and honey. He was offering a land with corn, wine, bread and vineyards. When he realized he was not convincing them to make a treaty, his last attempt was with INTIMIDATION AND DOUBT. He warned them to beware of Hezekiah. He would tell them to trust God, but no god had been able to stop the Assyrian king. Did they think theirs would?

Ask Yourself

- Thinking of yesterday's journal, do I feel as though God isn't big enough to get me out of the enemy's plan?
- Do I feel as though my situation is too big for God, so I need to handle it, finding my own way out?
- What lies of intimidation and doubt do I hear?

Ask God to show you how to stand strong. Ask Him to show you the strategy Satan has used before, is still using today and that is affecting you.

⚡ DAY 46 ⚡

Are You Acting or Reacting?

Today, I am thankful for: _____

_____

_____

Today's Scripture Reading Is Isaiah 37:1-38

When Hezekiah heard what was being said and done, he responded by doing something amazing. He went into the House of the Lord and sent the three men to the prophet Isaiah. They told the prophet what was going on, while King Hezekiah's waited before the Lord, trusting God to vindicate him. He didn't want to just "react"; he wanted a word from the Lord.

God answered Hezekiah, telling him not to be afraid of the threats being made, they were actually threats against Him, and He would fight for Hezekiah. *"Behold, I will send a blast upon him, and he shall hear a rumour, and return to his own land; and I will cause him to fall by the sword in his own land"* (verse 7).

Do you see what was happening here? The King of Assyria wanted the Israelites to surrender because of his threats and the rumors he spread, and now he was reaping what he had sowed, reacting to the rumors he heard.

Going Deeper

Look at both sides of this situation and figure out which side you see yourself on.

Ask Yourself

- Am I feeling like King Hezekiah, hearing rumors that have been spread against me?
- What is my reaction when I hear that there is a rumor going around behind my back?
- Do I react, or do I go to God first and find out how He wants me to respond?
- When I am being faced with confusion, manipulation, fear, and doubt, do I act on impulse, or do I search the Word of God for an answer?
- Do I seek godly counsel?
- Do I respond like Hezekiah when I am faced with a situation or do I just react?
- Am I feeling like the King of Assyria, reaping what I have sowed in the past?
- If so, what am I reaping because of what I have sowed?

_____

_____

_____

Ask God to show you what side you are on. Ask Him to help you not react impulsively to a given situation, but instead, to respond to the actions around you by seeking Him for an appropriate answer.

✂ DAY 47 ✄

What Is My Prayer Like?

Today, I am thankful for: _____

_____

_____

Today's Scripture Reading Is Isaiah 37:14-35 and Psalm 46:10

This part of Isaiah gives more detail about King Hezekiah's response and his prayer concerning the King of Assyria. Hezekiah received a letter from a messenger, read it and then went to the House of the Lord and spread it out before God. *Spreading it out* refers to "breaking it apart" or "dispersing it," or it can be translated as "to lay it open." In other words, he took what he was facing and laid it open before God, exposing to God in prayer what he was seeing and how he was seeing it.

The outline of Hezekiah's prayer was simple and yet powerful. He started by telling God that He had all glory, that He was the only true God, and that He had created the heavens and the earth. He then asked God to open His eyes and ears to what the King of Assyria was actually doing.

God answered Hezekiah and showed him what the enemy king was doing. One by one he was destroying all the surrounding nations, burning the gods that others served. Hezekiah asked God to save his people from the evil hand of the King of Assyria so that all the kingdoms of the earth might know that He was the true God.

In his prayer, Hezekiah said to God, "I know who You are." Then he opened up and told God how he saw the situation, and he ended his prayer with this powerful thought: "The battle is Yours, God." He wanted God to save His people so that others could see how He moves. He didn't ask God, "What do You want me to do?" He didn't even ask God how He would save them? In essence, he had enough faith in God that he just prayed, "Save us, and I don't need to know how or when."

God responded to Hezekiah and told him He would indeed save him and His people: *"For I will defend this city to save it for mine own sake, and for my servant David's sake"* (verse 35). God was saying: "I will save you for my reputation and for the promise I made to David in 2 Samuel 7.

Ask Yourself

- Do I go to God with how I see reality and see what He has to say, or do I just react?
- Do I want God to save me and intervene for *my* reputation or for *His*?

_____

_____

_____

Ask God to show you the deepest part of your heart, to show you where you want any glory or honor when He moves.

✄ DAY 48 ✄

What Is the Purpose of Judgement?

Today, I am thankful for: _____

_____

_____

Today's Scripture Reading Is Isaiah 42:13-25 and Matthew 6:33

This whole section is on the judgment of God. His judgment is there to open prison doors, and, in turn, will set us free. Once we are free, we can then go and set others free.

It's hard to give someone something you don't have. We cannot help others see what we don't see ourselves. Matthew 6:33 says, *"But seek ye first the kingdom of God and his righteousness."* We have to be willing to seek God first by applying what we see written in the Word to our own personal lives and to put into practice what we hear being preached.

Isaiah 42:18-20 speaks of the people being blind and deaf. Verse 22 speaks of them being robbed and spoiled, being snared in holes, and hid in prisons. Why are they in this condition if God is leading them? What would cause them to end up in this condition? A little further on the chapter gives us a clue as to why this was happening. It says that God gave them up to be robbed and spoiled because they would not walk in His ways and be obedient to His laws. It was because of their disobedience that God's anger burned against them. He was the one battling with them *"with fire round about,"* and they didn't even know it. It burned them, and they still chose not to apply it to their hearts.

Ask Yourself

- Do I apply and prove the message preached, or do I just leave having heard a good message?
- Does my disobedience to God's Word open a door for the thief to come into my life?
- Am I at war to the point that I am getting physically injured (being burned), yet I still don't change my ways and apply it to my heart? (Being stubborn and disobedient gets you burned.)

_____

_____

_____

Ask God to remind you of the last thing He told you to do and start to apply that to your heart immediately.

❧ DAY 49 ❧

Do I Understand a Fast?

Today, I am thankful for: _____

_____

_____

Today's Scripture Reading Is
Isaiah 58:1-4

This whole chapter, which we will discuss over the next two days, explains a true fast and the power it holds. God wanted Israel to know what fasting was. He first told them what they were doing, then He told them what He expected of them. Today we will examine how the people of Israel perceived a fast.

God spoke through the prophet Isaiah, urging him to be honest with the Israelites and call out their transgressions. Try to put yourself in their place. If it happened today, you would be in church and a prophet would begin to speak. He (or she) would say:

"You pray to God daily. You appear eager to know His ways. You think your outward actions are right, but inside your heart you are not listening to what God is telling or showing you. You ask God for answers and direction, and you appear eager for Him to show up, but deep down you question if God even hears your prayers and sees you humble yourself in a fast."

God responded to the Israelites by saying, "I see your fasting, this religious prayer thing you do, while, at the same time, exploiting your workers. *Your* fast ends with quarrels, strife and striking each other."

They asked God if He saw their fast and heard their prayers, and He responded by saying that He saw their lifestyle and how they interacted with others. In their head, they were praying and asking for God's help, but in their heart and actions, they still did exactly what they wanted.

Ask Yourself

- Do I feel as though God hears my prayers?
- Are my mouth and my heart going in different directions like the Israelites?
- Do I outwardly seek God by going to church, doing Bible study, journaling or even praying, but inwardly doing what I want and justifying myself?
- Am I doing what God requires of me and waiting on Him?

_____

_____

_____

Ask God to show you where your heart, which is inward, is not lining up with your lifestyle, your outward actions.

☙ DAY 50 ❧

What Is God's Version of a Fast?

Today, I am thankful for: _____

_____

_____

Today's Scripture Reading Is Isaiah 58:5-12

Yesterday, we saw what the Israelites' perception of a fast was. We tend to look at a fast as humbling ourselves. We crucify the flesh by temporarily giving up something that reminds us to pray. In verse 5, God asked them, *"Is it such a fast that I have chosen? A day for a man to afflict his soul?"* In other words, should I really accept this? Today, we will see what God considers a fast to be. I will paraphrase it, making it easier to understand, but please follow along in your Bible.

God's fast consists of A LIFESTYLE OF (verses 5-7):

- **Freeing those wrongly imprisoned:** Do I stop someone when I hear them wrongly accuse another person?
- **Lightening the burdens of others:** Do I help others when I see a need or someone struggling, or only if it benefits me?

- **Setting the oppressed free:** Do I help others get free from guilt, depression, etc.?
- **Removing the chains holding people down:** Am I helping others in their struggle with bondage?
- **Sharing food and shelter:** Am I sharing revelations and breakthroughs I receive with others, feeding them spiritually?
- **Covering the naked:** Do I cover the shame of others?
- **Not hiding from your own flesh:** Am I honest with myself and transparent with God and others?

What happens when we live the lifestyle Jesus wants us to live? Verse 8 starts with the word *THEN*. That leads you to think that this section of scripture is dependent upon the first part happening. If you live the lifestyle revealed in verses 6-7, *"THEN shall thy light break forth as the morning, and thine health shall spring forth speedily: and thy righteousness shall go before thee; the glory of the* LORD *shall be thy reward. Then shalt thou call, and the* LORD *shall answer; thou shalt cry, and he shall say, Here I am."* IF you're vulnerable and deal with yourself and help others, your reality will start to change to noonday instead of darkness.

Ask Yourself

- What part of this lifestyle of fasting am I not fulfilling?

_____

_____

_____

Ask God to show you how to start with one little lifestyle change today so that you can begin living the lifestyle of a fast.

❦ DAY 51 ❧

What Is My Call?

Today's Scripture Reading Is Jeremiah 1:4-10

In verse 5, God said to Jeremiah, *"Before I formed thee in the belly I knew thee; and before thou camest forth out of the womb I sanctified thee, and I ordained thee a prophet unto the nations."* We all have a call on our lives! Once Jeremiah realized that he was called as a prophet, his response today could sound something like this: "Oh, my goodness, I don't know how to be a prophet." But God went on to correct Jeremiah. "Don't talk like that. You are not to be a prophet using *your* words but using *My* words."

Jeremiah's response created an inability within himself to yield to God, because he didn't think what God was saying was even possible. Just like Jeremiah, we are all given a calling in life before we are born, and the things that God gives us at birth He never takes back.

Because Jeremiah didn't feel worthy of such a call, his words could also have been an excuse. We don't know for sure, but put yourself in his shoes. Do you know the calling on *your* life? Do you feel as though it is within your ability? If Jeremiah's weakness was his mouth, then in that weakness, God was (and still is) strong!

Think about your own weaknesses. Are you even aware of them? Are you willing to be vulnerable and let God shine through your weaknesses?

Ask Yourself

- Do I know my calling in life?
- Am I walking in that calling?
- What weaknesses do I let get in the way of God using me?
- Do I allow God to shine strong through my weaknesses?

_____

_____

_____

_____

_____

_____

Ask God to show you what your calling in life is. Then start allowing yourself to be used in that area.

℘ **DAY 52** ☙

How Do I Prepare for Battle?

Today, I am thankful for: _____

_____

_____

Today's Scripture Reading Is Jeremiah 1:17-19 and 2 Corinthians 10:3-5

In Jeremiah, this whole section in my Bible is labeled "God's Protection of Jeremiah," but notice that it begins: *"Thou therefore gird up thy loins, and arise, and speak unto them all that I command thee: be not dismayed at their faces, lest I confound thee before them."* "But," God warned Jeremiah, "if you become dismayed, distraught, worried and cower in fear, then I will allow them to overtake you." He went on to say that He was protecting Jeremiah and that his enemies would rise and fight against him, but they WOULD NOT prevail. We all want to be in that place during any battle so that we will not be overtaken by the storm.

The storms of life can get rough and overtake us if we aren't prepared and don't know how to fight. The key to winning the battle is understanding the fight. It is a mental game. There is a battle that takes place in our mind, and we are told in the Scriptures: *"bringing into captivity every thought to the obedience of Christ"* (2 Corinthians 10:5).

The first thing God told Jeremiah was: *"Gird up your loins."* This term was also used for the belt of truth we are to employ when putting on the whole armor of God (see Ephesians 6:14). The way you wear your belt is by getting in the Word for yourself. This is the first piece of armor, and it affects how you wear the rest of it.

When you get in the Word, you begin to hear God's voice and learn His heart, by having a relationship with Him. Then, when God tells you to speak, you become obedient and begin to speak because you know His voice. But what if you don't know His voice? What if you feel you can't recognize His voice while you're in the storm? What do you do in the middle of your emotions rising? Will you heed another voice over God's? When we heed our emotions or other voices over God's, we are headed toward a losing battle.

Ask Yourself

- Do I recognize God's voice?
- Do I get in the Word for myself?
- Am I wearing my belt of truth and dressed for battle?

_____

_____

_____

Ask God to help you have a new thirst for His Word. Then get into the Word daily so that you will be able to hear God's voice loud and clear.

❧ DAY 53 ❧

Is God Being Falsely Accused?

Today, I am thankful for: _____

_____

_____

Today's Scripture Reading Is Jeremiah 2:1-37

As you read this chapter, you will see that God told the people why He was judging them and why His anger was aroused. In verses 13-17, we gain a clear picture of what happened. They had committed two evils (sins): 1). They had forsaken God, the living water, and 2). They had dug their own cisterns that were broken and could not hold water.

The passage goes on to describe the consequences of the evil they had committed. God told them that they had brought this on themselves by forsaking Him. He continued to tell them about the wrongs they had done. He said He had planted a good vine from a good seed, but they had turned into a strange vine.

God then asked them, "Why do you complain and accuse Me, when you are the ones who have rebelled?" This is something I believe a lot of people could still do today. We tend to falsely accuse God because we feel innocent and think that His anger should turn from us.

What are ways we can commit these same two evils today? How do we forsake God and dig our own cisterns? What might we put before God today? We could put money, power, title or even a position before Him. We can even put sleep, comfort or time before spending time with God. We tend to forget that God brought us out from bondage (which is our form of Egypt) to the Promised Land (which is the blessing we can currently experience). We tend to walk away from God and still blame Him when things go wrong.

Ask Yourself

- Have I walked away from God, and yet I blame Him for the storms that are coming against me?
- Do I blame God for allowing bad things to happen?
- Do I spend time with God when things are going well or only when things are going bad?

_____

_____

_____

Spend some time asking God what is happening with the storms in your life.

℘ **DAY 54** ℘

Does God's Word Take Root in Me?

Today, I am thankful for: _____

_____

_____

Today's Scripture Reading Is Jeremiah 4:1-6 and Mark 4:1-20

When you hear a message preached, does it take root in your heart, changing your actions? Do you comprehend the message? God's Word is intended to penetrate our heart and change our behavior. That, in turn, will change our reality! There are four ways people can respond to the Word of God:

1. **On the Wayside**: This is when the Word is stolen from you IMMEDIATELY after you hear it.

2. **Stony Ground**: This is when you hear the Word and receive it, but when pressure comes your way, you are offended.

3. **Thorns**: This is when you hear the Word, and it takes root, but demonic influences or the struggles of this world choke the Word, and you don't bear fruit.

4. **Good Ground**: This is when you hear the Word, and you are able to bear the fruit of it in your life.

I want us to spend a moment meditating on #3 in this list of ways we can respond to God's Word. According to Jeremiah, if we have a hard heart, the Word of God will fall among thorns. The next verse shows us that we must be willing to circumcise our heart by taking away the foreskin. The foreskin is the covering or top layer. It is the self-protection we throw up so that we don't get hurt! We say that things don't bother us when they do. We self-reject before others can reject us. If we are being serious but people laugh, we tend to play it off as a joke, to protect ourselves and not be vulnerable.

Ask Yourself:

- What has hardened my heart to this point?
- Could it be sin, anger, unforgiveness, wounds left undealt with, abandonment, etc.?
- Spend some time and list what has hardened *your* heart.

_____

_____

_____

_____

Ask God to help you remove the things you listed above from your heart. When you remove these things, that will allow the Word of God to penetrate and take root in your heart.

৶ DAY 55 ৾

Do I Teach My Children Well?

Today, I am thankful for: _____

_____

_____

Today's Scripture Reading Is Jeremiah 5:1-10

The chapter begins with God looking for a righteous man. If a righteous man could be found, God would forgive Jerusalem. He went on to say in the next verse, *"And though they say, The LORD liveth; surely they swear falsely"* (verse 2). God saw their hearts! He tried to correct them, but they REFUSED to receive correction. Their faces hardened as rock, and they REFUSED to repent and turn back to Him. They didn't really know or understand His ways.

What really sticks out to me is that what they had taught their children affected them, whether they realized it or not. God was good to them, and yet they continued to turn to idols. He compared these children to well-fed, lusty stallions going after their neighbor's wife.

As you make your way through life, there is more at stake than just your own salvation. You are always teaching or mentoring others—for good or for evil. God was willing to forgive these people, but He held them accountable for what they had taught (or not taught) their children. They seemed to have a lifestyle of "Christian Talk," speaking of loving God, but, at the same time, swearing falsely. Their lifestyle didn't match what they said about themselves. Your children or others you mentor will do what you *do* and not what you *say*!

Ask Yourself

- By looking at my children or those I've mentored, can I see what I have taught them?
- Did I teach them to forsake God and lean on themselves or to lean on God?
- For example, if they had trust issues, can they trust in God or even a man under God to provide for them?
- Do they "have to" provide for themselves?
- Did I teach them to self-provide or to trust in God?
- Did I teach them to suppress their emotions or to be open?
- Have they become numb, thinking that no one will understand?

_____

_____

_____

Ask God to show you how to teach your children or those you are mentoring according to His Word and not your own perceptions.

✄ DAY 56 ✄

What Is My Promise from God?

Today, I am thankful for: _____

_____

_____

Today's Scripture Reading Is Jeremiah 5:11-19

Because Israel and the house of Judah dealt treacherously against God, He would send a mighty nation to eat their harvest (the bread meant for their children), eat their flocks and herds, eat their vines and fig trees and destroy the fenced cities they trusted in. They had dealt treacherously by lying and denying God because they didn't know Him. Still, the promise here was that even though God was sending this adversary against them, He WOULD NOT make a full end of them. This experience WOULD NOT completely destroy them. God was trying to wake them up by showing them what was in their own hearts.

"When your people say, 'Why has the LORD our God done all these things to us?' then you shall answer them, 'As you have abandoned (reject-ed) Me,' [says the Lord,] 'and have served strange and foreign gods in your land, so you will serve strangers in a land that is not yours' " (verse 19, AMP). Their reality of serving strangers was a mirror image of their

heart, to show them what they were doing to God. We live under the New Covenant now, and everything is done internally, written on our hearts. We speak from our heart, creating our own reality!

Our reality today is STILL a mirror image to show us what is currently in our hearts. We speak what we feel and believe, and therefore we create our reality by our words. As an example: in my head I know that God's Word says I'm blessed and everything I put my hand to will prosper, but in my heart, do I really believe it? Do I really believe that God will bless everything I put my hands to? I have walls up that stop me from trusting and putting my career or abilities in God's hand. I do what I can see, but I speak out of the walls and fears I have within my heart. I could say things like, "I'll do this, but it's not going to work," or "When one thing breaks, everything breaks." My head may be speaking the words, but my heart is feeling something very different.

The Scriptures say that we speak out of our heart, and our words have creative power. Our heart dictates our speech, which, in turn, dictates the reality we live in. The only way to change reality, then, is to change our heart!

Ask Yourself

- What words must I change to change my reality?

_____

_____

_____

Ask God to help you change your heart so that you can produce a different harvest as you plant seeds through your speech.

⚝ DAY 57 ⚝

Do I Have a Lifestyle or a Ritual?

Today, I am thankful for: _____

_____

_____

Today's Scripture Reading Is Jeremiah 7:1-12 and Deuteronomy 8:19-20

Jeremiah 7:3 says, *"Amend your ways and your doings, and I will cause you to dwell in this place."* Reading in different translations may help with understanding what "amending our ways" means. The Amplified Version , for instance, states, *"Change your ways and your behavior, and I will let you live in this place."* If we are willing to change our lifestyle, THEN God causes us to dwell in the place He has chosen.

What is *this place* He is referring to? The people were standing at the gate of the Lord's house when this conversation was taking place. We all want to abide in the secret place of the Lord, in His presence, under His wings, being protected and in peace. But there is a lifestyle that God requires of us if we are to dwell in *this place*.

- We are NOT to trust in lying words. We cannot assume that we are protected just because we are physically in the Lord's temple. A ritual or a place doesn't give you any rights or freedom, but a relationship with Christ does. In this context, these people had worship rituals with NO relationship.

- We are to execute judgment and honesty, treating everyone fairly and making right decisions.
- We are NOT to oppress the stranger, the fatherless or the widow. Don't exploit anyone or be cruel to anyone.
- We are NOT to shed innocent blood. We can do this by gossiping about others and killing their reputations with other people. We can also belittle people to make ourselves look better.
- We are NOT to walk after gods of our own hurts! For example, do we tend to heed the voice of rejection, fear or even betrayal over the voice of God?

This is the lifestyle God requires of us, if we are to dwell in the Promised Land Scriptures refer to! We can have Heaven on Earth manifesting in our reality!

Ask Yourself

- What part of my life needs a lifestyle adjustment?

_____

_____

_____

_____

Ask God to show you what, in your life, doesn't fit "His" requirements and then change it to meet His expectations.

℘ DAY 58 ℘

Does God Test Me?

Today, I am thankful for: _____

_____

_____

Today's Scripture Reading Is Jeremiah 9:1-16

In verse 7 God said, *"I will melt them, and try them."* The Amplified version says, *"Behold, I will refine them [through suffering] and test them."* We must ask ourselves why God allows this and what the purpose of it is. As you read, you will see the progression. We go from evil to evil, because we don't know God. We live in a state of deceit, because we refuse to know God. Then it goes on to say, *"Therefore, God will melt us and try us."* This is done on purpose to wake us up. He wants to get our attention and show us that we don't know the true Jesus; we only know *about* Him.

This passage refers to our tongue as an arrow (see verse 8). We speak peace with our neighbor, but our heart harbors a trap. Inwardly, we are wanting to see them fall. This is the person God puts through the refining fire to get the impurities out of their heart! The purpose of the fire is to burn out the "stuff" that is in our heart that is not of God.

They refused to know or understand God. We can also see that they were in this place of testing because they:

- Had forsaken the Law (which was the Word of God)
- Had not obeyed God's voice
- Did not walk after God (which was their lifestyle), but followed after their own heart and after other gods

Their heart laid traps.

Ask Yourself

- Am I going through hard times because of my own actions?
- If God is trying to get my attention and wake me up, what does He want me to see or hear?

_____

_____

_____

Ask God to show you why you may be in a season of refining fire in your life. Be open to see if it is by your own doing or what God may be trying to show you.

ɢ **DAY 59** ℞

Can the Promised Land Manifest Today?

Today, I am thankful for: _____

_____

_____

Today's Scripture Reading Is Jeremiah 11:1-5

God spoke to Jeremiah and told him to tell everyone, *"Cursed be the man that obeyeth not the words of this covenant which I commanded your fathers in the day that I brought them forth out of the land of Egypt"* (verse 3-4). You might ask, "What did He command them?" In verse 4, He commanded: *"Obey my voice, and do them, according to all which I command you: so shall ye be my people, and I will be your God."* From this we can gather that if we are disobedient to God's voice, we live under a curse!

But what if we are obedient? Then, obviously, we are not put under a curse, and, instead, we will receive what the following verse promises, a place where God performs all that He has promised, a land flowing with milk and honey, the Promised Land!

The Promised Land was the land of Canaan given to the children of Israel as an inheritance after they had come out of bondage in Egypt, but can the Promised Land manifest today? Absolutely! The manifestation of the Promised Land today is contingent upon our obedience to God's voice.

We are constantly obeying someone's voice. It may be God's voice, but it may also be the voice of fear. It may even be the voice of rejection, pride, betrayal or abandonment. Is the Promised Land, the manifestation of the promises of God's Word, a reality in your life today? If so, that's great, but if not, why? It is a question worth asking.

Ask Yourself

- Am I obedient to God's voice?
- Am I doing what God tells me in His Word?
- Or am I doing what my hurts and built-up walls tell me to do, so that I don't get hurt again?

_____

_____

_____

_____

_____

Ask God to show you the truth about whose voice you sometimes heed over His.

⚮ DAY 60 ⚯

How Do I Respond?

Today, I am thankful for: _____

_____

_____

Today's Scripture Reading Is
Jeremiah 11:18-23

Jeremiah got a check in his spirit that someone was plotting behind his back to kill him. They had political, economic, religious and personal reasons to be against Jeremiah and the message he was preaching. Jeremiah took the matter to God.

You may not be physically plotting to kill someone, but you can easily kill someone's reputation with others by warning them to be careful around that person. If we do this because we want others to know who that person is in our eyes, then we just killed that person in the eyes of the individual we are addressing. We just destroyed the chances of God using that person to minister to them, because we have killed their trust in them.

Put yourself in Jeremiah's place. You have a gut instinct that someone is talking about you, killing your reputation with other people. What do you do? There are two major possibilities:

You can become "soul-led." This will put you in the driver's seat and take you straight into action. You will immediately go out and start trying to clear you own name, vindicating yourself. You may even shed innocent blood in the process, killing the reputation or image of the person you think is killing you. This puts you on the throne with God, and you only see in part!

You can become "Spirit-led." In this case, you go straight to prayer. You don't pray a repetitious-type prayer, but, instead, a warfare-type of prayer. You go to prayer, asking God to expose the truth, for the truth will set both people free! Then, you sit back and allow God to vindicate you. This leaves God on the throne, and He sees the picture as a whole!

Ask Yourself

- When I have the feeling I am being talked about, do I respond by being soul-led or Spirit-led and why?

_____

_____

_____

_____

Ask God to help you become Spirit-led in all of your reactions to life's issues.

✄ DAY 61 ✄

Do I Question God?

Today, I am thankful for: _____

_____

_____

Today's Scripture Reading Is
Jeremiah 12:1-17

Jeremiah started questioning God. "Why is this happening?" "Why do they prosper?" "Why do they look happy when their actions aren't right?" He continued to tell God that He was on their lips but far from their hearts or minds. Jeremiah's complaint was that God had tried *him* but why not *them*?

God responded to Jeremiah, *"So, Jeremiah, if you're worn out in this footrace with men, what makes you think you can race against horse? And if you can't keep your wits during times of calm, what's going to happen when trouble breaks loose like the Jordan in flood?"* (verse 5, MSG). Jeremiah was communicating with God the fact that life was not fair, but he wasn't in a battle yet. He was tired of the fight between the men of the land. This was the reality he saw. But God compared Jeremiah to racing horses and the floodwaters of the Jordan, telling him that he was worried and tired just looking at the physical.

The truth we all need to know is that we are not warring against flesh and blood but against demonic spirits. If we spend our time focused on a person and not praying for that person, what will we do when a spiritual attack comes?

No, life is not fair. But we build our character when we rise above the storms and fight from heavenly places with Jesus. This is our rightful position. While it is fine to go to God and ask questions, just ask Him to help you rise above every storm and every adverse situation so that you can renew your strength in Him.

Ask Yourself

- What situations in my life have I questioned God about?
- Am I willing to let go and let God raise me up above the storms of life?
- What is God wanting to show me in this storm, so that I will not have to circle the same mountain over and over again?

_____

_____

_____

_____

_____

_____

Have a serious conversation with God, and keep an open mind to start seeing situations and people differently.

❧ DAY 62 ❧

Is God Continually Speaking?

Today, I am thankful for: _____

_____

_____

Today's Scripture Reading Is
Jeremiah 13:1-14

Here we see Jeremiah's reactions to God's voice. Look at the way in which it all unfolds. God spoke to Jeremiah to do something that seemed unusual, and Jeremiah was obedient to do exactly what he heard God say. As soon as his actions were taken, *"according to the word of the LORD"* (verse 2), you can see the Lord speaking to him a second time.

God now told Jeremiah that He wanted him to hide the girdle he had put on by the River Euphrates. The good thing was that Jeremiah did not question God about this. Instead, he was obedient and hid it, just as God had said.

The very next verse declares, *"And it came to pass after many days ... ."* God now wanted Jeremiah to go and retrieve what he had hidden. This must have seemed odd to Jeremiah, to first hide it and then to go and find it, but his actions reflected obedience to what God had spoken to him.

After Jeremiah did this, God told him what it all meant. Very often we want God to tell us the end before we are willing to act. We want to know what it all means before we will take one step. But God's direction for our life is much like this conversation. If we are willing to be obedient to His voice, He will tell us every step to take. We just need to start moving in an action of obedience to what He tells us.

What would have happened if Jeremiah had hidden the girdle in a different place or found it sooner than God wanted? What if his curiosity had gotten the best of him, and he had gone ahead of what God was saying? Careful obedience is important.

Ask Yourself

- What is God telling me to do?
- Am I obedient to what He says or do I add what I think to what God has said?
- Am I obedient and patient enough that God can ultimately reveal to me the meaning and understanding of what is happening around me?

_____

_____

_____

_____

Ask God to help you heed His voice and be obedient to act upon what you hear. As you do, His voice will grow louder and more frequent in your life.

⚡ DAY 63 ⚡

Does God Accept Me?

Today, I am thankful for: _____

_____

_____

Today's Scripture Reading Is
Jeremiah 14:1-22

This chapter begins with the Israelites in a drought. God gave Jeremiah a word of knowledge about the people and the drought. There was no rain, so people were covering their heads from shame, wanting God to do something *"for thy name's sake"* (verse 7), even though they knew they had backslidden and had sinned against Him. They called God *"the hope of Israel, the saviour thereof in time of trouble"* (verse 8). Can you believe their nerve? They had NOT REPENTED of their sins, and yet they expected God to move on their behalf—just because they were praying and calling on His name.

Then God spoke: *"They have loved to wander; they have not restrained their feet. Therefore the LORD does not accept them; He will now remember [in detail] their wickedness and punish them for their sins"* (verse 10, AMP). He went on to say: *"When they fast, I will not hear their cry; and when offer burnt offering and an oblation, I will not accept them: but I will consume them by the sword, and by the famine, and by the pestilence"* (verse 12). He was referring to people of faith. They knew how to fast and to perform other religious acts, but God did not accept them. They went as far as to acknowledge their sinful ways before God, but they DID NOT REPENT.

As a Christian, do you go to God only when your back is against the wall? Do you do the things a Christian should be doing and yet feel as though your prayer hits a wall, and you aren't being answered? If so, study verse 10 on your own and with an open heart.

Notice the word *therefore*, which means "because of what just happened." Therefore, God will not accept them. Why? Because they loved to wander and did not refrain their feet. This phrase *loved to wander* could signify not being rooted in a home church. Not refraining their feet could mean they had no self-discipline, standards, or convictions to undergird their lives.

Ask Yourself

- Do I find myself in verse 10?
- If so, where?
- What do I need to change, so that God can accept me?

_____

_____

_____

Ask God to show you how to live a lifestyle that is sweet and acceptable to Him.

❦ DAY 64 ❧

Are God's Judgements Always Redemptive in Nature?

Today, I am thankful for: _____

_____

_____

Today's Scripture Reading Is
Genesis 15:1-17 and Jeremiah 15:1-7

We should all know that God's judgements are redemptive in nature. He is patient, He extends grace, and He doesn't judge our sin until it's full.

Genesis records the fact that God gave Abram a vision and told him that He would afflict the Israelites for four hundred years. Then, in Genesis 15:14, God said, *"And also that nation, whom they shall serve, will I judge: and afterword shall they come out with great substance."* God was sending the Israelites temporarily into Egypt, because the time for judging was not yet full. After He had judged the Egyptians, He would release His people, and they would come forth with great possessions.

Jeremiah recorded judgment on the nation through a drought, pestilence and sword, and all of that because their actions imitated that of their leader. God said (concerning His people), "Because they have forsaken Me and gone backward, I will stretch out My hand and destroy them" (see verse 6). Because He is God, He is able to sort through people and destroy those who fail to repent and turn from their own ways.

Judgement is always intended to wake us up and get our focus back on God. We read yesterday that God didn't accept the behavior of the people, and the dry season sent to their lives was a judgement meant to wake them up. All of God's judgements are designed to bring us back to Him, to wake us up to our need of repentance!

Ask Yourself

- What is God waking me up from?
- What is He trying to show me?

_____

_____

_____

_____

_____

_____

Ask God to show you His redemptive hand at work in this season in your life. Call out to Him and let Him rain down on you His blessings.

⌘ DAY 65 ⌘

Whom Do I Trust?

Today, I am thankful for: _____

_____

_____

Today's Scripture Reading Is
Jeremiah 17:1-10 and 1 Corinthians 11:31-32

Jeremiah 17 begins by saying that sin was engraved on the hearts of the people. We know that we speak from the abundance of our heart and create our reality through the words we speak. Our words are a mirror of our heart. Too often, in our minds, we trust God but, in our hearts, we trust what our eyes see. We trust the hurts and lies we have experienced in the past. This passage also tells us who is *"cursed"* and who is *"blessed,"* and what their reality looks like. It ends with our heart: *"I the LORD search the heart, I try the reins even to give every man according to the fruit of his doings"* (verse 10).

Let's compare the reality of someone who trusts in man against the reality of the one who trusts in the Lord (according to Jeremiah 17). If I am trusting in Man (verses 5-6), I am under a curse. I draw strength from people, not God. My heart is focused on people, not God. Therefore, I look like a shrub in the desert. I don't see anything good. I live in a dry place in the wilderness. I live in a salt land, a place that is barren with no fruit.

If I am trusting in the Lord (verses 7-8), I am blessed. I have hope. I am a tree planted by living water, rooted in Christ. I am well rooted and planted in the Word and in a church. I don't see the heat coming because I don't focus on negative circumstances. My leaves stay green because the negative reality does not affect me. I'm not careful in the year of drought and, therefore, have no anxieties. I never stop producing fruit since my life stays consistent.

We are judged according to our heart. If you examine your reality, you will see your heart.

Ask Yourself

- What is happening in my reality?
- Does my reality look more like the one who trusts in man or the one who trusts in God and why?

_____

_____

_____

_____

_____

_____

_____

Ask God to show you where you are trusting in man and how to transfer that trust to Him.

⚓ DAY 66 ⚓

Do I Take Vengeance When I Am Slandered?

Today, I am thankful for: _____

_____

_____

Today's Scripture Reading Is
Jeremiah 18:11-23

Jeremiah prophesied to the people of his day and told them to repent from their evil ways and return to God, but they chose not to. Instead, they continued to go after their own plans and to follow the stubbornness of their own heart. They even schemed against Jeremiah because they believed the false prophets in the area. They attacked the true prophet with their words and refused to give heed to anything he said, and they spread false rumors about him.

Jeremiah responded by taking all of this to God in prayer. He told God, "Look what they are saying about me. They are digging a hole and trap for me to fall into. They are twisting what I say and saying things I didn't say at all. They are setting me up to fall, and they think they are on top."

He went on to tell God that his intentions were good. "I tried to get them to see the error of their ways and to repent, so that You would turn away Your wrath," he protested. "Now judge *them* and vindicate *me!*"

Put yourself in Jeremiah's place. His reputation was being trashed in front of the king. How would you have reacted? How do you react when, like Jeremiah, rumors are being spread about you, and your reputation is being slandered to some authority figure? What is your natural response? I am not asking how you hope you would respond, but what would be your true actions?

Ask Yourself

- There are two ways to respond to slander: 1). Stop and pray or 2). Attempt to defend myself. Which of these is my first response and why?

_____

_____

_____

_____

_____

Ask God to help you have the mature response of stopping to pray. Allow Him to vindicate you rather than taking matters into your own hands.

⚕ **DAY 67** ⚗

Do I Speak Against Others?

Today, I am thankful for: _____

_____

_____

Today's Scripture Reading Is
Jeremiah 20:1-10

In the very first verse of Jeremiah 20, Pashur is identified as the son of a priest and Chief Governor in the House of the Lord. As the Chief Governor, he had oversight of the temple, the temple guards, entry into the temple courts and more. Unfortunately Pashur didn't like Jeremiah, so he smote, or hit, the prophet and had him locked up. What Jeremiah said bothered Pashur so he thought maybe this would quiet the hated prophet.

What was Jeremiah saying that was so objectionable? He was speaking against idolatry, the worship of false gods. Because Pashur was in charge of the temple (the local church), Jeremiah's prophetic word made him very uncomfortable, and this was how Pashur responded, by locking him away.

Think about prophetic words and ministries today. If there is a word or a ministry that convicts you or makes you uncomfortable, how do you respond to it?

- Do you attempt to discredit that person or ministry by spreading rumors about them?
- Do you try to set up roadblocks for them to hit a wall and stop?
- Do you accept the word or ministry and change, if that is what God requires of you?
- Do you pray and let God handle the situation?

Your response shows your character, so Pashur's response and actions didn't look good.

Ask Yourself

- What are my actions when I am convicted by a prophetic word and why?

_____

_____

_____

_____

_____

_____

_____

_____

_____

Ask God to reveal to you how He sees your actions, and if you need to change them to better represent Him.

✄ **DAY 68** ✎

Am I Fighting God?

Today, I am thankful for: _____

_____

_____

Today's Scripture Reading Is Jeremiah 21:1-14 and Galatians 6:7-9

For many chapters, Jeremiah had been prophesying judgement if the people failed to turn from their evil ways, repent and return to God. Here, in the first verses of chapter 21, notice that as soon as the judgment started to hit, the people ran to Jeremiah (because he knew God) and asked him to pray for them. They wanted God to deal with them according to who He was and not according to their actions. They wanted grace and protection from Him, but notice God's response.

God said to them that the first thing He would do is to make their weapons ineffective. They would be ineffective in battle because they were not fighting men, but God Himself. The chapter closes with this summary: *"I will punish you according to the fruit of your doings."* God had given them a lot of grace and warnings that this day would come.

Apply this to today's reality. Many people seek wise counsel, desire for God to give them a word or a warning that something is coming their way, but all the while, they have no intention of changing their behavior. They keep on their way, expecting a gracious and forgiving God they can walk over. Then, when the bad times come, and it's time to face the consequence of their action, they quickly run to God for help.

People want and seek temporary relief from the harvest of the bad seeds they have sown, but God said, *"Whatsoever a man soweth, that shall he also reap"* (Galatians 6:7). Because of their disobedience, not heeding God's voice and doing what He has asked, they find themselves battling. They think they are fighting some enemy, but, in truth, they are fighting God Himself.

Ask Yourself

- Do I only go to God for temporary help?
- Are my weapons "ineffective"?
- Am I fighting the enemy or God?
- Considering Jeremiah 21:8, which says, *"I set before you the way of life* [obedience] *and the way of death* [disobedience},*"* what is my choice?

_____

_____

_____

_____

Ask God to show you the truth of the battle you are in. Is it actually against God Himself?

℘ DAY 69 ℜ

Am I Being Obedient?

Today, I am thankful for: _____

_____

_____

Today's Scripture Reading Is Jeremiah 22:1-4

God instructed Jeremiah to tell the people, *"Hear the word of the LORD"* (verse 2), and the chapter goes on to list all those who were to listen to this word. The prophet addressed the king, his servants and all the people who entered in by the gates of the city. He went on to enumerate things that God required of the people:

1. To do what was right.
2. To help the oppressed and those being robbed — physically and spiritually.
3. To do no wrong.
4. To do no violence.
5. Not to shed innocent blood.

Most of these are self-explanatory, but I want to spend a moment discussing the shedding of innocent blood. How might we shed innocent blood today? We can kill someone spiritually or even emotionally. We can kill someone's reputation or even someone's hope. One way we can do this is through gossip. We can cause other people to not trust or like the person we are talking about, and, in so doing, kill them spiritually.

Another way we can do much harm is by speaking carelessly to someone seeking help on how to handle a certain situation. If you are the person seeking help, don't kill the other person's image even as you take their advice. If you are the one giving the advice, you have the opportunity either to kill or restore the hope of the person involved. In that moment, you are the way they see Jesus! Handle that situation with care!

Ask Yourself

- What do people think about Jesus when they look at me?
- Which one of the five things listed do I need to obey and why?
- How or in which way do I disobey any of these five instructions?

_____

_____

_____

_____

Ask God to show you if you have not been obedient to His Word so that when people look at you, they will see Jesus.

How Am I Disobedient?

Today, I am thankful for: _____

_____

_____

Today's Scripture Reading Is Jeremiah 22:5-12, Deuteronomy 29:25-26 and 5:1-21

Yesterday we read that we are all called to be obedient, not just our leaders, but what happens if we are disobedient? And what is considered "disobedience?" When we are disobedient, we become a desolation and a wilderness. To us, this is spiritually speaking, although it had a physical outcome in Old Testament times.

But what does God consider "disobedience?" The text goes on to say that they had forsaken the covenant of the Lord and had worshipped and served other gods, which is idolatry. So, what is the covenant they forsook?

Deuteronomy 29 refers to a covenant God made with the people as they were leaving Egypt. Deuteronomy 5 shows that this covenant contained the Ten Commandments. Follow these commandments, and it will keep you from returning to Egypt, which is spiritual bondage. If you abide by the Ten Commandments, you will make it through to the Promised Land.

Since we are a New Covenant people, the covenant now lies within our hearts. Consequently, you have to look at the Ten Commandments and the inside of your heart at the same time. Do you live with the commandments as a guardrail in your life, with the help of the Holy Spirit guiding you? The Israelites worshipped idols. An idol is any inward god that we heed over the voice of the true and living God.

In Jeremiah 22:21, God spoke to the prophet, but he didn't hear Him. Then God told him that this had been his lifestyle since his youth. Who did he heed over God's voice?

Ask Yourself

- What priorities do I have and what voices do I heed over God's?
- As a special challenge, find a New Testament scripture to back up each of the Ten Commandments. Then meditate on them to see if you are obedient or disobedient to God in your current lifestyle.

_____

_____

_____

_____

Pray and ask God to open your eyes to see if there are areas that He's convicting you of. Do you need to be more obedient in this area?

℘ DAY 71 ✎

Am I a Good Influence?

Today, I am thankful for: _____

_____

_____

Today's Scripture Reading Is
Jeremiah 23:1-4, 2 Timothy 1:7
and 1 John 4:18

In this section of Jeremiah, God was addressing the pastors over the flock. You may immediately think, "Well, I'm not a pastor," but what does a pastor do? You may not be over a church, but you have influence over others. We all influence someone every day by our words and our actions. In turn, we judge others by the fruit of their life, whether we can trust them, get advice from them, or if we want to be mentored by them.

For example, you may not want to learn from someone how to be debt free or build or rebuild your credit if the fruit of their life is credit card abuse and debt collection agencies. You may not go to a person and confide in them for advice if you see that the fruit in their life is gossip and an inability to keep secrets. God said that He would visit the evil of the bad shepherd and bring the people to a good shepherd.

According to verse 4, God said, *"And I will set up shepherds over them which shall feed them: and they shall fear no more, nor be dismayed, neither shall they be lacking."* What does this mean to those of us who are not pastors? We are all called to imitate or be like Jesus, so others should see Jesus in our lifestyle. We should influence them the way Jesus did. This means that we all feed the flock in one way or another.

Do you feed others fear or love? Are you feeding them God's unconditional love or man's conditional love? Are you feeding others shame or condemnation? When you influence people, do they leave in confusion about how they should act, or do they leave well-grounded in God's Word? Do you feed them Jesus, the Well of Living Water that never runs dry, or after you have talked, do they leave still depressed and anxious?

Ask Yourself

- What kind of influence am I?
- Which type of shepherd am I? Am I a good shepherd who feeds others Jesus or am I a bad shepherd who jumps into negativity along with others?
- What is the fruit in my life?

_____

_____

_____

_____

Ask God to teach you how to be the shepherd He called you to be.

∅ **DAY 72** ∿

What Is a Prophet's Fruit?

Today, I am thankful for: _____

_____

_____

Today's Scripture Reading Is Jeremiah 28:1-17 and 1 Samuel 15:23

Jeremiah 28 is all about the false prophecy of a man named Hananiah and the consequences of it. The people had been taken captive for seventy years because of their idolatry, but Hananiah told them that God would restore them in just two years. This must have excited the people. Jeremiah then confronted the situation by admonishing Hananiah. At first, it sounded like Jeremiah was agreeing with Hananiah: *"Amen: the LORD do so: the LORD perform thy words which thou hast prophesied"* (verse 6). But then Jeremiah said, *"When the word of the prophet shall come to pass, then shall the prophet be known that the LORD hath truly sent him."* In other words, you can tell if you are listening to a true prophet, like Jeremiah, or a false prophet, like Hananiah, by which words come to pass. In chapter 25, we saw that Jeremiah had already been prophesying for many years what was coming—even when the people were not happy to hear it.

Notice what happened to Hananiah in the last few verses of the chapter. Jeremiah confronted him again: *"The Lord hath not sent thee; but thou makest this people to trust in a lie"* (verse 15). According to verse 16, making people believe a lie is teaching rebellion against the Lord Himself. And *"rebellion is as the sin of witchcraft"* (1 Samuel 15:23)!

Think about yourself. You may not be a prophet, but we all hear from God and can then relay to others the character of the God we believe in by how we speak about Him and how we live for Him.

Ask Yourself

- Do I have a perception of God only from hearing others preach or by being in His Word for myself?
- Do I tell people what they want to hear or do I tell them the truth in love?

_____

_____

_____

_____

_____

Ask God to help you live a lifestyle that displays the fruits of who He truly is and not just a false perception of Him.

℘ DAY 73 ℘

Why Am I in a Hard Spot?

Today, I am thankful for: _____

_____

_____

Today's Scripture Reading Is Jeremiah 29:1-14 and 21:1-10

Chapter 29 starts with a letter Jeremiah wrote to the people who had been taken captive. This captivity was God's way of redeeming them. What? Could God sending them into captivity have been a good thing? Yes, God's anger was against them, and they should have been destroyed. His way of saving them was to take them out of their city and into captivity. He told them: *"And unto this people thou shalt say, Thus saith the Lord; behold, I set before you the way of life, and the way of death. He that abideth in this city shall die by the sword, and by the famine, and by the pestilence: but he that goeth out, and falleth to the Chaldeans that besiege you, he shall live, and his life shall be unto him for a prey"* (Jeremiah 21:8-9).

Jeremiah 29 explains to us more of what God expected of the people while they were in captivity. He told them to build houses, to dwell there, to plant gardens and to eat the fruit of them (see verse 28). So, even in the hard times, when our reality isn't what we think life should be like, we should make the best of it and increase on every side.

The Israelites were also to do this: *"And seek the peace of the city whither I have caused you to be carried away captives, and pray unto the LORD for it: for in the peace thereof shall ye have peace"* (verse 7). Who are you praying for? Are you praying for the peace of your city?

God went on to say, *"And ye shall seek me, and find me, when ye shall search for me with all your heart"* (verse 13). God had to become the most important part of their life. They were being punished, or judged, in a pagan city for idolatry and not heeding God's voice. That punishment or judgment was meant to rid their lives of idolatry once and for all.

Ask Yourself

- Thinking about a hard time I am having, what is it God could be stripping from me?
- What is it that I tend to turn to before turning to Him?

_____

_____

_____

_____

_____

Ask God to show you if there are things you turn to before Him, what they are and why you do it. Then, as He reveals them to you, clean out your heart so you can turn to Jesus before you have to hit rock bottom.

⚡ DAY 74 ⚡

Who Do My Actions Affect?

Today, I am thankful for: _____

_____

_____

Today's Scripture Reading Is
Jeremiah 29:15-32

In today's lesson, Jeremiah is still referring to false prophets and what becomes of them. We read yesterday what a false prophet is, someone who teaches a lie and, in turn, causes others to rebel against God. But as you read today's lesson, who did Shemaiah's actions truly affect the most? THEY AFFECTED HIS DESCENDANTS!

Verse 32 says, *"Therefore thus saith the LORD; behold, I will punish Shemaiah the Nehalamite, and his seed: he shall not have a man to dwell among this people; neither shall he behold the good that I will do for my people, saith the LORD; because he hath taught rebellion against the LORD."* Because this is such a serious matter, we all have to take a step back and look closely at our speech and our actions. If we are, in any way, teaching rebellion against the Lord, that will affect the reality our children live in.

God said that no man would dwell among His people or see the good He would do for them. Shemaiah's actions would affect the reality of the generations to come.

Your actions also affect more than just yourself, the same way your life is affected because of your forefathers before you. The Scriptures teach us to repent of our forefather's iniquities, a twisted mindset against God. It is from that mindset that we talk and act, and those words and actions teach others around us to do the same.

Ask Yourself

- Whom do my actions and speech affect?
- What ways do I need to change so that I can teach others to turn to God?
- What speech do I need to change that doesn't glorify God?

_____

_____

_____

_____

_____

_____

_____

_____

Ask God to show you the ways in which you are affecting those around you—negatively or positively.

❧ DAY 75 ❧

What Is the New Covenant?

Today, I am thankful for: _____

_____

_____

Today's Scripture Reading Is
Jeremiah 31:27-34 and Hebrews 8:7-13

When you read both the Old and New Testament passages, they say almost the exact same thing. The Old Testament speaks of what was to come, while the New Testament speaks of what is now available. The Old Covenant is the one God made with the Israelites when He brought them out of Egypt. He gave them the Ten Commandments. These were guidelines of how they should live, to prevent them from returning to Egypt, and they were read in front of the people at certain times of the year, to teach the people what was expected of them.

The New Covenant is more internal. The commandments of God are now written on our hearts instead of on stone tablets. We are all born with a deep knowing of right from wrong. We are all to share Jesus with our neighbors and the world around us. We are no longer to teach just the rules and regulations of the Old Covenant; we are to teach a relationship with Jesus Christ. Think about your heart and the Ten Commandments.

If you watch a small child, you don't have to tell them that something is wrong; they automatically look around, fearful that they are being watched because something they are doing just feels wrong. We, as adults, if we're not careful, can come to ignore the convictions we used to feel. The more you ignore these convictions and go against what is written on your heart, the smaller that feeling of conviction becomes. Eventually you get to a place where you are numb to the convictions you once felt. When you don't heed those convictions, your heart hardens, eventually not feeling conviction at all.

Ask Yourself

- If I don't feel convictions any more, why not?
- What was the last conviction I felt that I compromised with?
- If I do feel convictions, which conviction do I feel that I need to pay more attention to?

_____

_____

_____

_____

_____

If you no longer feel convictions, ask God to let you start feeling them again. Ask Him to let your convictions grow stronger and stronger.

๛ **DAY 76** ๛

Do I Keep My Word?

Today, I am thankful for: _____

_____

_____

Today's Scripture Reading Is Jeremiah 34:12-22

God said to the Israelite people, *"I made a covenant with your fathers in the day that I brought them forth out of the band of Egypt, out of the house of bondmen, saying, At the end of seven years let ye go every man his brother an Hebrew, which hath been sold unto thee; and when he hath served thee six years, thou shalt let him go free from thee: but your fathers hearkened not unto me, neither inclined their ear. And ye were now turned, and had done right in my sight, in proclaiming liberty every man to his neighbor; and ye had made a covenant before me in the house which is called by my name"* (verses 13-15). He was telling them that He was pleased that they had done what He asked.

Each of us has also made covenants or promises to God. At some point in our life, we have gotten caught up in the emotion of everyone around us, in the excitement of prophecies or sermons preached, and have made promises to ourselves with God as our witness. It is so easy to say we will do something different when we leave church, and we all strive to live differently afterward, but we are not always successful.

This passage shows that the people polluted God's name when they turned and did what they were not supposed to do. This is dishonoring to God, and it goes on to say what comes into your life as a consequence of breaking such a covenant: *"the sword,"* which could be symbolic of war; *"the pestilence,"* which could be symbolic of diseases and sicknesses; *"the famine,"* which could be symbolic of starvation, hunger or a season of drought. Plus, we are handed over to our enemies. In other words, when we break our covenant with God, we fall under a curse.

Ask Yourself

- Do I do what I say I will do?
- Do I make impulsive promises that I know I will never keep?
- What have I promised myself or God that I would do and haven't done yet?

_____

_____

_____

_____

_____

_____

Ask God to bring to your remembrance anything you have promised to do but have not yet done.

ॐ **DAY 77** ॐ

What Is Simple Obedience?

Today, I am thankful for: _____

_____

_____

Today's Scripture Reading Is Jeremiah 35:1-19 and James 4:17

This chapter of Jeremiah is entitled "The Rechabites' Obedience." These people were offered wine, and they refused it because they had been taught by their fathers not to partake of wine. This prohibition extended to other things as well: *"Nor shall you build a house or sow seed or plant a vineyard or own one; but you shall live in tents all your days, that you may live many days in the land where you are sojourners (temporary residents)"* (verse 7, AMP). They were in full obedience to the authority figure/s over their life. My study notes refer to this as being "similar to a Nazarite vow," and the Rechabites had obeyed it for nearly twenty years. They were not about to disobey what had been commanded of them just to please men (even Jeremiah). These were not people-pleasers; they were simple obedient followers.

Are you simply obedient to what God has spoken to you? Do you heed the Holy Spirit when you hear Him say, "No, don't do that?" You may not always understand the big picture, but how obedient are you to the commands over your life?

James 4:17 says, *"So any person who knows what is right to do but does not do it, to him it is sin"* (AMP). When we are disobedient to the conviction of the command over us, we are in sin. PERIOD!

Jeremiah went on to compare the obedience of the Rechabites to the disobedience of the people of Judah. Their disobedience to God's Word and to His prophets brought disaster upon them. The Rechabites' obedience, on the other hand, brought them to a place that they will ALWAYS have someone who stands before Jesus. This was an amazing legacy to leave behind, a legacy of SIMPLE OBEDIENCE!

Ask Yourself

- Whom do I obey?
- Do I obey God's Word and the authorities over me?
- Do I obey by conviction, or do I base my actions on what others around me are doing?
- Does the influence of those around me shake my level of obedience?

_____

_____

_____

Ask God to let you hear His voice only and to obey what you hear. Ask Him that your convictions and actions of obedience be not shaken by the influence of others around you.

❧ DAY 78 ❧

Do I Seek Just What I Want To Hear?

Today, I am thankful for: _____

_____

_____

Today's Scripture Reading Is Jeremiah 37:1-21

The chapter starts with the king, his servants and his people not listening to the Word of the Lord that Jeremiah spoke. They refused to heed his warnings over and over concerning the captivity that would come because they had disobeyed God. Interestingly, when things started to go wrong, the king and his prophet went to Jeremiah and asked him to pray to God on their behalf. Jeremiah prayed and received a word for them, but they didn't like the word they received and falsely accused Jeremiah of being on the side of their Chaldean enemies and had him thrown into prison.

The king got Jeremiah out of prison and secretly asked him to come to his house to get a word from God, but Jeremiah received the same word as before.

I have several thoughts on this chapter, but I want to focus on just one of them. These people didn't want to heed any of Jeremiah's words because they would have to change how they lived. They knew that he was a proven prophet, and they wanted God's help, but when they didn't get the word they wanted, they had him imprisoned, then secretly asked for another word, hoping it would be different.

How many times do we not like the consequences of our actions, and yet we won't change? We often go to people we know have a relationship with God for prayer, hoping they can get a different word than the one we currently have received.

Ask Yourself

- Do I expect God to do for me if I continue to seek counsel but don't heed the words He speaks to me?
- Do I ever seek wise counsel secretly to see if I can hear what I want because I am afraid of the consequences if other people knew?

_____

_____

_____

_____

_____

Ask God to help you heed the words He speaks to you and not keep seeking someone who will tell you only what you want to hear.

Do I Understand God?

Today, I am thankful for: _____

_____

_____

Today's Scripture Reading Is Jeremiah 40:1-16 and Deuteronomy 28:1-68

Jeremiah was being freed from imprisonment by Nebuzaradan, a captain of the guard. Nebuzaradan blamed God for all of the disastrous evil that was occurring. I absolutely love Jeremiah's response. He told the man that God was doing it because the people had sinned and not obeyed His voice. We tend to always think that God is the One who's in control, but do we truly understand who God is and what His Word says.

For instance, the Word of God says that we reap what we sow (see Galatians 6:7) and that we are made in God's image (see Genesis 1:27). He created the worlds by His words (see Genesis 1:3, 6 and 14), so if we are created in His image, then we create our reality by our speech. We "eat" the fruit of our lips (see Proverbs 18:20), and the power of life and death are in the tongue (see Proverbs 18:21).

Deuteronomy 28 lists the blessings we receive through obedience and the curses we put ourselves under through disobedience. "IF" we listen and do, "THEN" we get the blessings. "IF" we don't listen and don't do, "THEN" we bring ourselves under the curses.

Therefore, if I was being disobedient to something that God laid out in His Word, it would be unscriptural if I said, "God is allowing this to happen." The truth is that our disobedience is why our reality is what it is, and yet we often fail to recognize our disobedience. All we can see is that God is not intervening in our reality.

Ask Yourself

- Does my speech line up with the Word of God or does it actually contradict His Word?
- Do I have only head knowledge of the Word of God or do I have heart knowledge of His Word?

_____

_____

_____

_____

_____

_____

Ask God to give you a deeper understanding of His person and His characteristics.

☙ DAY 80 ❧

Do I Hold On To My Word?

Today, I am thankful for: _____

_____

_____

Today's Scripture Reading Is
Jeremiah 42:1-22 and Ecclesiastes 5:4-6

Here we see the people of Jeremiah's day approaching him, wanting him to seek the Lord for direction for them. Notice that they made a promise to obey God whether they liked the direction He gave or not. It took Jeremiah ten days of prayer to hear from God, and when He did speak, the message was for the people to stay put and boldly face the king they were afraid of.

Jeremiah said to them, *"Thus says the LORD, the God of Israel, to whom you sent me to present your petition before Him: 'If you will indeed remain in this land, then I will build you up and not tear you down, and I will plant you and not uproot you; for I will relent and be satisfied concerning the disaster that I have inflicted on you [as discipline, and I will replace judgment with compassion]. Do not be afraid of the king of Babylon, whom you now fear [as if he were deity]; do not be afraid of him,' says the LORD, 'for [he is a mere man, but I am the living, omniscient God and] I am with you [always] to protect you and to deliver you from his hand. And I will show you compassion, so that he will have compassion on you and restore you to your own land' "* (Jeremiah 42:9-12, AMP).

Then God gave them a warning: IF they disobeyed and left for Egypt, THEN the judgment they were currently experiencing would follow them. Ecclesiastes 5:5 declares, *"It is better that you should not vow than that you should vow and not pay"* (AMP). Our mouth often causes our flesh to sin. If we say things and then don't do them, that becomes sin.

Notice here in Jeremiah that God warned them about following what they saw manifesting in their reality over what He was saying. This makes me think of the Garden of Eden. Adam heeded what reality said (when he saw his wife eat of the forbidden tree and nothing happened to her) over what God had told him. God had said not to eat of that tree, and when Adam ate from it, because reality didn't look all that bad, he sinned against God. Jeremiah warned that "reality" often isn't what it seems.

Ask Yourself

- Do I follow reality or God? Why?
- Do I do what I hear God saying when I pray?

_____

_____

_____

_____

Ask God to show you the areas in your life where you heed reality over His voice.

What Are the Side Effects of Pride?

Today, I am thankful for: _____

_____

_____

Today's Scripture Reading Is Jeremiah 43:1-7

Yesterday, we saw how the people went to Jeremiah, seeking prayer and a word from God. Jeremiah told them what would happen if they stayed put and what would happen if they went to Egypt. Toward the end of chapter 42, Jeremiah was rebuking them because they wanted God's opinion, but they refused to obey it. They disobeyed because their reality (going to Egypt) seemed better to them.

Now we see that pride caused these men to claim that Jeremiah was speaking falsely. At this point, many of his words had proven him to be a true prophet because they came to pass. There are many side effects of pride, but I want to focus here on two of them. 1). Pride caused them to reject God's Word, and 2). Pride stopped them from recognizing that word as God's Word.

Notice in the storyline that they had wanted Jeremiah to seek God for a word, but then they denied that word when it came. Why? Inwardly, could they have wanted God to bless *their* plan and give His permission or His blessing to it? When God rejected their plan and insisted that they follow His plan, pride caused them to resist. Humility causes us to follow God's directions even when we don't feel like it or don't understand them fully.

Ask Yourself

- When I go to prayer, is it to get God to bless *my* plan or is it to get *His* plan so that I can follow it?

_____

_____

_____

_____

_____

_____

_____

_____

_____

Ask God to help you not to reject any word He gives you. Ask Him to help you see His plan for your life and not to be blind to it. Ask Him to help you see that His plan is always better than your own.

☙ DAY 82 ☙

What Is the Importance of Family Time?

Today, I am thankful for: _____

_____

_____

Today's Scripture Reading Is
1 Kings 4:1-34 and 5:1-18

Solomon was considered to be one of the wisest men who ever lived. He wrote parts of Proverbs, Psalms, Ecclesiastes and The Song of Songs (or Song of Solomon). God picked Solomon to build the Temple in Jerusalem even though David, his father, had desired to build it himself. God rejected David's plan because he was a man of war.

One of the aspects of Solomon's wisdom and character that really grabbed my attention appears at the end of chapter 5. When he was starting to plan for the temple construction and hiring the men who would do the work, he told them they could work for a month and then stay at home for two months. My study notes indicate that King

Solomon understood that the strength of the nation was directly proportional to the strength of the Israelite families. He understood and valued family time.

Do you value family time? Do you invest enough time and energy into your spouse and children? Do you value the strength of the family unit? Modern society as a whole devalues family time by telling us to do what is best for ourselves, but God Himself designed the family, and your children are with you only for a short season. Your spouse and children are your highest ministry calling.

Is family time a priority with you? Do your spouse and children know that you choose them over hobbies, sports, TV, your phone or even your friends?

Ask Yourself

- On a scale of 1 to 10, with 10 being the most, how much do I value my family time?
- Does my family know they are valued?
- By looking at my life from the outside, what would others say I value most and why?

_____

_____

_____

_____

_____

Ask God to open your eyes to see exactly what you value in life. Ask Him to help you prioritize according to His Word.

How Do I Handle Rumors?

Today, I am thankful for: _____

_____

_____

Today's Scripture Reading Is
1 Kings 10:1-13

The lesson begins with the Queen of Sheba hearing about the wisdom of Solomon and deciding to investigate to see if these rumors were true or not. I believe there is a concept here that we all need to catch. Whether Sheba was jealous, competitive, or just curious, at least she confronted the situation and took action. In these verses, we can see what she observed and her reaction to it. She questioned Solomon extensively, and he answered all of her questions. The result was that she went home an admirer of both Solomon and of his God.

There are rumors that circulate around you and me every day, and rumors can take several different forms. Rumors can get started when someone is simply venting, blowing off steam. Rumors can get started because of jealousy, anger, unforgiveness, pride, wounds or even the wrong perception people sometimes have. I want to focus on the queen's behavior versus Solomon's behavior:

Solomon was the one being talked about, and yet he didn't bother to go find people and try to clear his name. God vindicated him by allowing the queen to come and investigate what she had heard. The queen overheard rumors, and she confronted the situation by going straight to the source, to see if the rumor were true or not. In the process, her eyes were opened to the greatness of God.

Ask Yourself

- Which of these do I act like and why?
- Do I act wisely like Solomon did?
- Do I do what I need to do, following God and being obedient without going around trying to figure out what is being said about me?
- Do I allow God to vindicate me, or do I try to vindicate myself?
- Do I act like this queen did? When I hear a situation, do I find out the truth myself from the source before acting or making a judgment?
- Do I act like the people in between, spreading rumors about other people?

_____

_____

_____

_____

_____

Ask God to help you handle rumors correctly, confronting what needs to be confronted, and allowing Him to defend you in His timing.

❦ DAY 84 ❧

What Influence Am I Around?

Today, I am thankful for: _____

_____

_____

Today's Scripture Reading Is 1 Kings 11:1-13

In the beginning of this book, we see how God visited and appeared to Solomon on two occasions. Solomon was completely sold out to God. All he wanted in life was wisdom and discernment, so God added to him riches and honor. Now, however, things take a turn in chapter 11.

The chapter begins with Solomon loving *"many" strange* (or foreign) *women"* from nations that God did not approve of. Verse 2 declares: *"Of the nations concerning which the LORD said unto the children of Israel, Ye shall not go in to them, neither shall they come in unto you: for surely they will turn away your heart after their gods: Solomon clave unto these in love."* The influence of foreign wives would pull the heart of the Israelite men toward their false gods. Nevertheless, Solomon rebelled against the command of God, and his spiritual compromise opened the door of his heart to idolatry. *"For it came to pass, when Solomon was old, that his wives turned away his heart after other gods: and his heart was not perfect with the Lord his God, as was the heart of David his father"* (Verse 4). It didn't happen all at once, but over a period of years, but it happened. Perhaps it happened so slowly that Solomon didn't even see it coming until it was too late. In the end, he was making provisions for his wives's gods by building them altars.

God was angry at Solomon, of course, and declared that his son would inherit only a portion of the kingdom. He would receive that portion only because of God's promise to David. God would choose someone else to rule the rest of the kingdom.

Think about that! God had appeared to Solomon twice, and yet he allowed a foreign influence to turn his heart from God. His disobedience in the matter of marriage led to his downfall.

Ask Yourself

- What influence has God commanded me to stop, and I haven't put an end to it yet?
- Has that influence started to turn my heart to the point of making excuses or justifications as to why it's okay for me to sin?

_____

_____

_____

_____

Ask God to open your eyes to the influences around you and also to the type of influence you are to others.

༄ **DAY 85** ༄

What Is Disobedience?

Today, I am thankful for: _____

_____

_____

Today's Scripture Reading Is 1 Kings 13:1-34

God sent a prophet to tell the king that what he was doing with the altars and incense was wrong. The king invited the man to come to his house, but the prophet refused. God had told the prophet before he went not to accept any invitations to eat or drink in that city. The prophet had also been instructed to leave the city the same way he entered it. He did everything right and was on his way out of the city when a man approached him. He gave him the same offer the king had made, and again the prophet refused.

Now something very strange happened. The man who had approached him said, *"I am a prophet also as thou art; and an angel spake unto me by the word of the LORD, saying, Bring him back with thee into thine house, that he may eat bread and drink water. But he lied unto him"* (verse 18). The original prophet, not realizing that this was a lie, agreed and accompanied the man to his house.

While they were eating, a word from God came telling the prophet that he had been disobedient by not keeping the precise commandment God had given to him for this mission. Do you see what happened here? Notice that the prophet was obedient until the moment the other man had said he was a prophet too and that an angel had spoken to him and told him to invite the visiting prophet to his home and to host him. This was some serious deceit, and yet God held the prophet responsible for not having completely obeyed Him. He had known in his heart exactly what God had told him to do, and yet he allowed someone to convince him to do otherwise.

Ask Yourself

- In my heart, what has God told me to do?
- Am I obeying Him fully, or do I obey Him up to the point of someone else's interpretation of what He told *them* for me?
- Do I recognize the dangers involved in this?

_____

_____

_____

_____

Ask God to show you your true level of obedience and where you have not fully obeyed Him because of being influenced by the opinions of others.

⚶ DAY 86 ⚘

How Do I Face Fear?

Today, I am thankful for: _____

_____

_____

Today's Scripture Reading Is
1 Kings 19:1-8, Deuteronomy 8:3,
Matthew 4:4 and Luke 4:4

In 1 Kings 18, Elijah displayed the power of God to the many false prophets of Baal by calling fire down from Heaven. After displaying the power of the true God and discrediting their false gods, he went on to kill those false prophets. King Ahab was aware of all of this, and chapter 19 begins with him telling Jezebel, his queen, all that Elijah had done.

According to chapter 16, when the king married Jezebel, he consented to worship Baal along with her. Now she was hearing that her god had been mocked and all her prophets had been killed. The result was that Jezebel sent a message to Elijah saying that she would do to *him* what he had done to her prophets.

Hearing what Jezebel was saying put so much fear in Elijah that he ran for his life, hid under a juniper tree and prayed to die.

Exhausted, Elijah fell asleep, and after a while an angel came 1). To wake him up, and 2). To feed him, *"because,"* he said, *"the journey is too great for thee"* (verse 7). The strength Elijah received from eating what the angel provided sustained him for forty days.

He would still have to face the spirit behind Jezebel, and that was causing him real fear. As we see from Jesus' words, we cannot live by bread alone, but must live by the words that come out of God's mouth. You will never outlast and overcome an enemy by operating in the physical realm. You must be spiritually fed and supernaturally strengthened. When Jesus was tempted by Satan in the wilderness, He quoted Deuteronomy. We must learn to do the same.

Ask Yourself

- Where does the enemy throw fear at me, causing me to run?
- Do I seek God through His Word and pray for what He has to say about any fearful situation, or do I just run and hide?

_____

_____

_____

_____

_____

Thank God for His Word and ask Him to show you what part of it will sustain you and aid you in battle.

༄ DAY 87 ༄

Am I a Silent Accomplice?

Today, I am thankful for: _____

_____

_____

Today's Scripture Reading Is
1 Kings 21:1-16

A man named Naboth had a vineyard next to the palace, of King Ahab, and the king wanted that vineyard. He made Naboth two offers: He would either give the man an even better vineyard in exchange for his, or he would give him the full value of the vineyard. Naboth refused both offers. The vineyard was an inheritance from his father, and he didn't want to let it go. Ahab went home discouraged and angry.

When Jezebel noticed that her husband was depressed and not eating, she naturally asked him what was wrong. He told her: *"Because I spoke to Naboth the Jezreelite and said to him, 'Give me your vineyard for money; or if you prefer, I will give you another vineyard for it.' But he answered, 'I will not give you my vineyard'"* (verse 6, AMP).

Jezebel answered: *"Do you now reign over Israel? Get up, eat food, and let your heart rejoice; I will give you the vineyard of Naboth the Jezreelite"* (verse 7, AMP).

The story goes on to say that the queen wrote letters in the king's name and had Naboth killed so that her husband could take by force the vineyard he loved so much. Sure enough, as soon as he heard the good news of Naboth's death, he immediately acted to take possession of the vineyard.

King Ahab had to know that something underhanded was taking place. How could he report Naboth's "no" and hear Jezebel saying, *"I will give you the vineyard,"* and not know that she was up to no good. The king allowed Jezebel to use his name and his royal seal to make it appear to others as if *he* had written the execution orders. We might call him a silent accomplice in the murder of Naboth and the thief of that vineyard.

Ask Yourself:

- Am I a silent accomplice in some evil deed?
- Do I sit silently by and let someone else act, knowing that what they are doing will benefit me, while I can appear to be innocent in the matter?

_____

_____

_____

_____

_____

Ask God to reveal to you any areas in your life where you are sitting back as evil is accomplished and, thus acting as a silent accomplice.

⚡ **DAY 88** ⚡

Do I Face Judgment
Or Do I Run?

Today, I am thankful for: _____

_____

_____

Today's Scripture Reading Is
1 Kings 22:1-53

The king of Israel wanted to go to war, and he asked Jehoshaphat, King of Judah, to help him. Jehoshaphat's answer is interesting: *"Jehoshaphat said to the king of Israel, 'I am as you are, my people as your people, my horses as your horses.' But Jehoshaphat said to the king of Israel, 'Please inquire first for the word of the LORD'"* (verses 4-5, AMP). The king called for the prophets (four hundred of them) and asked them: *"Shall I go to battle against Ramoth-gilead, or should I not?"* They answered, *"Go up, for the LORD has handed it over to the king"* (verse 6, AMP).

But something must have hit Jehoshaphat's discernment because he then asked the host king, *"Is there not another prophet of the LORD here whom we may ask?"* (verse 7, AMP). The king replied, *"There is one more man, Micaiah the son of Imlah, by whom we may inquire of the LORD, but I hate him, because he never prophesies good news for me, but only evil"* (verse 8, AMP). Micaiah was called, and he related to the two kings a vision from God. He had seen the men of Israel scattered on the hillsides like sheep without a shepherd. He also revealed the lying spirit that had worked through the four hundred prophets.

Of course, the king of Israel didn't like this word, so he had Micaiah imprisoned and went off to war. Strangely, he disguised himself. Now if he believed the word of the false prophets, why would he have done that? Perhaps in his heart he knew that what they had told him was just what he wanted to hear. By disguising himself, he was actually acting on the word of Micaiah. But even though the king was disguised, a random arrow flew through the joints of his harness and wounded him so badly that he died.

Ask Yourself

- Do I hearken to a true word with wise counsel, or do I seek counsel from those I know will tell me what I want to hear?
- Do I disguise myself and try to escape judgment?

_____

_____

_____

_____

_____

Ask God to show you if you truly face judgment or run from it? Ask Him to give you the strength to face whatever is ahead of you.

Am I Obedient?

Today, I am thankful for: _____

_____

_____

Today's Scripture Reading Is
2 Kings 3:1-27

King Jehoram, son of Ahab and Jezebel, along with King Jehoshaphat of Judah and the king of Edom decided to go to war against the rebel king, Mesha of Moab. On their way to the battlefront, they ran out of water and were in danger of perishing. So they determined to seek out a prophet of the Lord. The man they found was Elisha.

The first thing Elisha asked them for was a minstrel, or musician. He wanted to worship God. When the music had started, the hand of the Lord came upon him, and he was able to tell them how to escape their current dilemma. Worshiping God for who He is, approaching Him with thanksgiving, brings you into His presence. Worship shifts your atmosphere!

Now notice what God told these kings to do first: *"Make this valley full of ditches"* (verse 16). They had not said a word to Elisha about water. They had only asked him to tell them what would take place in the coming battle, but God knew their need of water. The kings were obedient and dug the ditches, and the next morning, those ditches were full of water. That water refreshed them for the battle to come.

Notice what God told them would happen if they dug ditches. Even though they would not see any wind or any rain, the valley would be full of water. You don't have to know *how* God will move on your behalf; you just need to be obedient to what He asks of you!

Ask Yourself

- What is God asking me to do?
- Am I willing to do what He is asking of me, even if it doesn't seem to make sense?

_____

_____

_____

_____

_____

_____

Ask God to give you the strength to be obedient in all the areas where His Spirit is nudging you.

❦ DAY 90 ❧

Do I Give God Everything I Have?

Today, I am thankful for: _____

_____

_____

Today's Scripture Reading Is
2 Kings 4:1-7

Yesterday, we read how those three kings dug ditches by faith, and God filled them with water. They couldn't see how He would save them, but He did. In today's lesson, the wife of one of the sons of the prophets went to Elisha and reported that her godly husband had died and left the family with debts. If those debts could not be paid, the creditor would take her two sons as slaves. She, too, was in a desperate situation. Sons were everything to a family in those days. Without them, there was no succession. Think of Ruth and Naomi and their dilemma. Without husbands or sons, they had nothing to sustain them.

When this woman asked Elisha for help, he responded, *"What hast thou in the house?"* (verse 2). He was referring to something of value that she could sell to pay the debt. All she had, she said, was a little pot of oil. He told her to borrow as many empty vessels as she could from her neighbors and, then, behind closed doors, she was to pour her oil into each of those vessels until they were full. The woman left and did as he had said.

In the physical, pouring a little oil into an empty vessel wouldn't make it multiply, but that was her place of obedience and faith, the place in her heart where God could multiply what she was offering Him. And He did. He multiplied her oil to the point that she could pay off the debt and live on what was left over.

This makes me think of the little boy who offered Jesus five fish and two small loaves of bread. That small lunch fed five thousand people and there were twelve baskets left over. God is not limited to what we have in the physical! All God needs from us is our willingness and obedience.

Ask Yourself

- What is it that I can offer to God?
- Am I willing to offer what I have? If not, why?

_____

_____

_____

_____

Ask God to give you strength to be obedient to offer up to Him what He asks of you.

Author Contact Page

You may contact Crystal Callais by email at:

maintainingfreedom@yahoo.com

www.ingramcontent.com/pod-product-compliance
Lightning Source LLC
LaVergne TN
LVHW011327080426
835513LV00006B/222